INTERNATIONAL GRAPHIC DESIGN, ART & ILLUSTRATION

Editor: YUSAKU KAMEKURA

Publisher: RECRUIT CO., LTD.
Production: RECRUIT CREATIVE CENTER

Printing: TOPPAN PRINTING CO., LTD.
Distributors: RIKUYO-SHA PUBLISHING, INC.
ZOKEISHA (USA) INC.

編集長 ——————————— 亀倉雄策

編集アシスタント ——————— 菊池雅美

アートディレクター ————— 亀倉雄策

デザイナー ——————————— 水上 寛
アシスタントデザイナー ——— 加藤正巳
　　　　　　　　　　　　　廣田由紀子
プリンティングディレクター —— 小嶋茂子
英訳 ————————————————— ロバート・ミンツァー

発行 ——————————— 1990年3月1日
定価 ——————————— 3,200円（本体3,107円）
発行所 ————————— 株式会社リクルート
　　　　　　　　　　〒104 東京都中央区銀座8-4-17
　　　　　　　　　　TEL.03-575-7074（編集室）
発行人 ————————— 位田尚隆
制作 ——————————— リクルートクリエイティブセンター
印刷 ——————————— 凸版印刷株式会社
用紙 ——————————— 特漉NKダルアート 日本加工製紙株式会社
発売 ——————————— 株式会社六耀社
　　　　　　　　　　〒160 東京都新宿区新宿2-19-12 静岡銀行ビル
　　　　　　　　　　TEL.03-354-4020 FAX.03-352-3106

世界のグラフィックデザイン, アート & イラストレーション

クリエイション

編集――亀倉雄策

発行――株式会社リクルート
制作――リクルートクリエイティブセンター

印刷――凸版印刷株式会社
発売――株式会社六耀社

Editor ———————— Yusaku Kamekura

Editorial assistant ——— Masami Kikuchi

Art director ————— Yusaku Kamekura

Designer ————————— Yutaka Mizukami
Assistant designers ——— Masami Kato
                        Yukiko Hirota
Printing director ———— Shigeko Kojima
Translator ————————— Robert A. Mintzer

CREATION No.4 1990
Publisher ————————— Recruit Co., Ltd.
                        8-4-17 Ginza, Chuo-ku, Tokyo 104, Japan
Production ——————— Recruit Creative Center
Printing —————————— Toppan Printing Co., Ltd.
Distributors ————— Rikuyo-sha Publishing, Inc.
                        Shizuoka Bank Bldg., 2-19-12 Shinjuku, Shinjuku-ku, Tokyo 160, Japan
                        TEL. 03-354-4020 FAX. 03-352-3106

                        Zokeisha (USA) Inc.
                        51 East 42nd Street New York N.Y. 10017 USA
                        TEL. 212-986-3120 FAX. 212-986-3122

CONTENTS──目次

Cover: JEAN-MICHEL FOLON

表紙：ジャン＝ミッシェル・フォロン

JAPANESE CULTURAL CROSSBREEDING 異種交配と新文化

Yusaku Kamekura 亀倉雄策

Foreign designers are said to be involved in over 200 projects currently in progress in Tokyo. They are also taking part in numerous projects in outlying cities across the country, although exact numbers are more difficult to glean in the latter instance. In scope their endeavors are of great variety: architecture, interior design, product design, graphics. For Japanese business firms, engaging the services of foreign designers is perhaps quite understandable. First, in an area that inherently aims to anticipate the future lifestyles of a national populace, the foreign designer is able to satisfy Japanese tastes to a T. Second, the hiring party benefits from the publicity that inevitably accompanies news of a foreign designer's participation in a project. Meanwhile, the foreign designer too reaps his rewards from such arrangements, since Japanese companies tend to allow the non-native considerably more creative freedom than is normally granted to a local designer. This peculiar phenomenon is likely to continue yet for quite some time...until the day when the Japanese once more acquire enough self-confidence to create culture and lifestyle for themselves.

On occasion I am taken by a childish fantasy. Here is how it goes. As you may know, during the Tokugawa Period Japan sealed its borders from the outside world for over 250 years, roughly from 1600 to 1868, a phenomenon unparalleled in length in any other country at any other time. This feat was possible owing to the physical insularity of the Japanese archipelago, the absence of bordering nations and the homogeneity of the Japanese race. The era was one of enduring peace broken by no major wars to speak of, a situation which enabled Japan to carry on its own unique aesthetic forms undisturbed. In every realm—architecture, clothing, customs, music, dance, art, crafts—more than two centuries of isolation enabled nonessential elements to be discarded and essential elements to be preserved, eventually yielding a native cultural heritage of simple, refined sophisticaiton. This was a period of nationwide unification of style, an aesthetic style of noble character.

In my personal fantasy I often wonder what would have happened if this phase of national seclusion had endured for another 80 years, until 1948. How strange it would have been, like flinging open a long-sealed door and discovering a mysterious fairyland straight out of ukiyo-e prints. Travelers would have flocked in hordes from all over the world to see this attraction far more intriguing than Disneyland could ever hope to be.

Today Japanese lifestyle is at a major turning point. In urban areas traditional Japanese lifestyle has rapidly faded into the background to be replaced by Western living modes, which are undeniably more practical and comfortable. Naturally there are some diehards who persist in keeping to a purely Japanese way of life. To do so, however, requires tremendous outlays of funds plus a willingness to endure numerous inconveniences. Of particular interest, though, is the emergence and vast popularity of a hybrid

今、東京では、海外のデザイナーが関わっているプロジェクトが200以上進行中だという。しかも、東京だけでなく地方都市にも波及していて、その数字を正確につかむことは難しい。建築、インテリア、プロダクト、グラフィックと幅が広い。デザインというのは、その国の民衆の生活の歩みを先取りする作業だから、企業が民衆の嗜好を迅速にとらえて海外のデザイナーを起用する。至極当然なことである。しかもジャーナリズムが目新しいニュースに飛びつくから宣伝効果は上々だ。企業は外国のデザイナーということで、当然日本人の設計ならば実現出来ないものを実現させてくれる。こういった珍現象はまだまだ続くだろう。日本人が、新しい生活文化を確立し、自信を持つまでは続く筈である。

私は、時々こんな子供じみた空想をすることがある。徳川時代の鎖国は250年。世界に類を見ない長さである。それは、日本は島国で、どの国とも接していない単一民族国家だからであった。250年の間、これといった大きな戦はなかった平和な国だった。だから固有の様式美を完全に伝承していた。建築、生活、衣服、風俗、歌舞音曲、絵画、工芸そして階級制度。どれをとっても長い時代を経て無駄なものは捨て、必要性からくる簡素に磨き込まれた洗練がそこにあった。まさに見事なまでに使い込まれた文化の形態が完成していた。要するに国全体に様式の統一が行き渡り、格調高い美学を誇っていたといっていいだろう。

私の空想は、その鎖国を80年のばしていたらどうだっただろうかということである。そうすると1948年に、やっと開国するわけだ。まるで、神秘な、おとぎの国の扉を開けるようなものだ。すると世界にも類を見ない不思議な島国に、世界中からどっと旅行者が押し寄せるに違いない。あの浮世絵の世界が現実に動いているんだから、恐らくディズニーランドも顔負けというくらい世界の人気を独占するに違いない。

今、日本人の現実の生活は大きな転換期に突入している。日本式の生活様式は都会では影をひそめ、西洋式に急速に変わりつつある。理由は西洋式の方が合理的で住みやすいからだ。もちろん純日本人の生活を守る人もいる。そのためには莫大な費用と不便さに耐えなくてはならない。面白いのは、西洋式と日本式とを混ぜる雑種文化がはびこっているということだ。私はこの現象を一概になじる気はない。文化が大きく転換する過渡的現象に過ぎないからだ。同じように現在、日本で海外デザイナーのプロジェクトがたくさん進行しているのも、一種の文化転換期の過渡的現象という認識で私はとらえている。

デザインは、今や世界の情報の渦の中にある。日本が自国の文化と違った文化を求める声に、敏感に反応し、しかも経済の隆盛期をとらえて波に乗る。欧米の一流の建築家やデザイナーが新開拓地になだれ込むのも当然の成り行きである。しかも、日本の文化のなかに異種文化が強力に入り込む。そこにどんなたくましい文化が育つだろうか。ここのところが問題だと思う。問題というのは、欧米の一流の建築家やデザイナーが、果たして日本という土地の上に、本当に世界的な視点から見て一級の仕事を残してくれるだろうかという、この1点に絞って私は注目しているのだ。日本の甘い市場をうかがう彼等の心理の一隅に、

culture blending elements both Western and Japanese. This trend is one which I personally would not disdain outright, 'since culture itself is in essence a transitory phenomenon in a constant state of flux. In this respect, I view the current participation of foreign designers in local projects as one facet of Japan's ongoing cultural tradition.

In contemporary Japan the design profession is caught in a maelstrom: propelled by economic prosperity, it is being pressed from all sides to create culture different from Japan's native culture. Under the circumstances it is only natural that first-rate architects and designers from the West are flocking to Japan to seek new business opportunities, aided by the fact that Japanese culture is by tradition receptive to outside elements. The crux of the matter, however, lies in what type of culture eventuates from this hybridization process. What particularly bothers me is the extent to which these leading Western architects and designers are truly dedicated to producing their best results here on Japanese soil. Personally I sense that, deep down, these foreigners see Japan as an easy market for their services, a view tinged by a latent disdain for Japan. To them Japan may be no more than a place to reap huge profits, not a place where they are committed to creating an outstanding new culture. In many instances they may be satisfied to do second-rate work in Japan, content with the knowledge that their representative works will be produced and judged on their home turf.

Western designers invariably say that Japan is the easiest place in the world for them to work, that Japanese clients always grant them freedom to proceed as they please. At first this opinion might suggest that Japanese firms are extremely sympathetic to the foreign designer's needs. In reality, however, it demonstrates how the foreign designer recognizes the easygoing nature of the Japanese client. It also reflects the common disdain in which Japanese businesses tend to hold architects and designers of their own country. Both of these trends—the foreigner's skewed view of Japan and the enduring adulation of the Japanese for the West—trace all the way back to the opening of the nation over 100 years ago.

Is Japan today actually capable of creating a new culture for itself? And if it is, what kind of culture will this be? Rather than one which is purely Japanese or purely Western, I believe it will be a cultural hybrid. In any case, what is clear is that as culture develops it casts aside impurities and accumulates only what is necessary. This is why, under the present circumstances, it would not matter even if there were 500 projects involving foreign designers—the question would still remain as to whether their achievements would ultimately be passed on as culture, and for the most part I predict they will be tossed aside as expendable debris. Rather than see this happen, I sincerely hope that foreign architects and designers will come to possess the foresight and commitment to create a new and truly valuable culture here in Japan.

日本蔑視の潜在意識が全くないとは言い切れないものを、私は感じてならなかった。日本は彼等にとって利益を吸い上げる市場でしかなく、文化を打ち立てるという気概がまるでないとしたら問題である。二流三流の仕事を適当にやって、本当に自分の代表作といわれるものは欧米の地の上でしか残さないとしたら、日本蔑視も甚だしいということになる。

「日本は世界で一番仕事のやりやすい国だ。しかも自分の好きなようにやらせてくれる」と欧米のデザイナーが口を揃えて言う。この言葉は、いかにも日本の企業に理解があるように聞こえるが、逆に日本の企業の甘さが見抜かれて、さらに日本企業が日本の建築家やデザイナーを蔑視している事実を物語っている。日本が250年間の鎖国を解いた時点から、日本人蔑視が始まっていたのだ。そしてこの日本人の西洋崇拝は、日本人の心の隅に大なり小なり巣を作っていて、鎖国を解いて100年以上たってもまだ根強く生き続けている。

日本は、これから新しい文化を創れるだろうか。創るとしたら、どんな文化になるのだろうか。西洋でも東洋でもない文化が生れるだろうか。異種交配による新文化かもしれない。どっちにしても、文化というのは積み重ねのなかで不純物を捨て去り、必要な輝きを蓄積して後世に残るものなのだ。だから300でも500でも海外のデザイナーのプロジェクトが次々に実現するのもいい。そのなかから果たして文化として残るものがあるだろうか。そのほとんどが消耗品という名の残骸になるかもしれない。

優れた見識と熱意を持った建築家やデザイナーが、日本という国に新しい文化を打ち立てるというアイデンティティを持ってほしいと思う。そのアイデンティティこそが本当の文化を創る礎石になると私は信じている。

JEAN-MICHEL FOLON ジャン＝ミッシェル・フォロン

Giorgio Soavi ジョルジオ・ソアビ

With the arrival of winter each year, instead of a conventional raincoat Folon takes to wearing a white garment with an uncanny resemblance to a parachute. Every time he coughs or heaves a sigh, it flaps about as though he were poised to take flight. He wears it, he says, to protect himself against the thick fog of Milan, a city he frequently visits on business.

By his own admission, Folon himself lives in a world of fog and dreams. But he adds that these elements are essential to his creative process. "Dreaming seems to be my predestined fate," he explains. "That's why I live in a dream world rather than in reality.

"With most people," he further states, "dreams appear only in one's sleep. But in my case, dreams go on and on in endless succession, during both sleeping and waking hours."

Because he lives in a never-ending fog, Folon says his designs are rich in color and packed with unusual images. He adds that these traits are also characteristic of his personal life. "Though I was born in Belgium and now live in Paris, I don't live what could be described as a 'North European' lifestyle. Actually my life is more like that of Southern Europe, which is why I prefer the bright oranges, blues and greens of the south over the clear, cold colors of the north."

Folon says that the grandest color spectacle he ever saw in his life took place at Key West, Florida. "Key West has the most beautiful sunsets in the world," he asserts. "People come and sit on benches just to watch the sun go down. On this particular day, as the sun slowly slipped below the horizon, flames of color shooting in every direction, everyone applauded wildly. Then, as if responding to their enthusiasm, the sun gave an encore by seeming to retrace its path, though only for a moment, to repeat its performance. Whereupon everyone rose from their seats and offered the sun a thunderous round of applause! It was a truly unforgettable sight— and a spectacle unimaginable in a northern country."

Folon's early watercolors are filled with his love of color and dreams. They brim with the joie de vivre of one who is friend to the earth and to all humankind. In Folon's creative world, life is always worth living. His works are artistic portraits of a born optimist whose every day is marked by joy and fascination with life.

To hear Folon's views on life and art, I arranged to meet him at a restaurant in Milan. As we sat waiting for our meal to arrive, Folon opened three packages of breadsticks set out on our table and proceeded not to eat them but to play with them as he spoke about art as a living expression.

"What I would like to do," he began, "is to find a skilled baker and have him make me a large birdcage out of breadsticks, complete with a roof and a little door. Then I would put a bird inside and watch it fly from one post to another, singing happily. When it got hungry, it would start pecking on the cage and discover it was edible. As it ate more, the cage which held him prisoner would first weaken and then eventually crumble apart, letting the bird fly off in freedom. So you see," Folon concluded gleefully, "depending how you look at it, even breadsticks can be very useful. They can give a bird its freedom."

冬が来ると、フォロンはレインコートの代わりに、咳やため息をする度にヒラヒラする白いパラシュートのようなものを身につける。それは仕事で訪れるミラノの濃い霧から身を守るためである。彼は靄と霧と夢の世界に住んでいると言う。そしてそれが彼の創作の重要な要素なのだ。「夢を見るという使命を運命が僕に与えたらしい」と彼は言う。「だから、僕は現実的ではなく、ぼんやり暮している。眠っている時に夢がどこからともなくやって来るというのではなく、むしろ絶え間なく連続する感覚から次第にある形に落ち着くってことなんだ」「だから僕のデザインは、色彩が豊かで、さまざまな事件がいっぱいつまっている霧の世界だ。それは、僕の生き方を象徴している」「僕はベルギー生まれでパリに暮しているが、北欧型の生き方をしているわけじゃない。むしろ南欧的だ。だから僕の好きな絵も、僕の内と外に輝いている光も、北欧の絵画の冷たい澄みきった光じゃなく、オレンジ、ブルー、グリーンの南欧の光なんだ。僕にとって空は、僕のカラーのスペクタクルを陽気に盛り上げる雲のイメージだ。僕の記憶にある最高のスペクタクル、それはフロリダのキーウェストだった。そこにはベンチがあって、人々は夕焼けを見るために座る。ここの夕焼けは、この世で一番美しいからだ。そうして人々は、色彩の炎を発しながら沈んでいく太陽の奇跡を見て、狂ったように拍手するんだ。太陽は、既成の概念にとらわれない自由な発想の人々のアンコールに応えるように、ほんの少しの瞬間、元の道を引き返すんじゃないかな。そして再び輝くと、人々は感動の余りベンチから立ち上がって、熱狂的な拍手喝采を送るんだ」「それは忘れがたいスペクタクルだ。北の国では見ることの出来ない光景だね。この熱狂ぶりはイタリアでのマラドーナのシュートに対する拍手と同様だ。180度反対のものの見方、夢の解釈の仕方なんだよ」

だから、フォロンの初期の水彩画にはカラフルで夢見る雰囲気がある。地球の友人、我々の友人フォロンがぼんやりと暮してた色彩豊かな霧の世界には洗練されたデザインがあった。そこでは人生は正に生きるに値し、木々には実が熟し、しかも豊かな味わいを誇っている。それこそ一人の生まれながらのオプティミストの喜びと驚きの肖像なのである。

ここはミラノのレストラン「ジーラロスト」。フォロンは細い棒パンのグリッシーニの袋を3つ開けて、食べるかわりに手でもてあそびながら、生きた芸術の表現について語った。

「パン職人の名人を探して、彼にグリッシーニで大きな鳥籠を作ってもらう。屋根と小さな扉がついていて、小鳥を中にいれてやるんだ。小鳥はあっちに止まり、こっちに止まって楽しげに歌う。そして腹が空くと、籠の格子をつっついて食べられることに気付くんだ。そして食べられる牢獄はばらばら壊れ始める。もっと食べると小鳥は自由の身になって飛んで行く」「考え方によってはグリッシーニだって大変役に立つんだよ。小鳥に自由を与えるんだもんね」

1-8 Illustrations for Olivetti diary オリベッティ社ダイアリーのイラスト 1968

2

5

6

7

9 "All Directions" 「すべての方向」 1970

10 Illustration for Olivetti diary オリベッティ社ダイアリーのイラスト 1968

11 "Another Spring"「もうひとつの春」1970

12 "The View" 「光景」1970

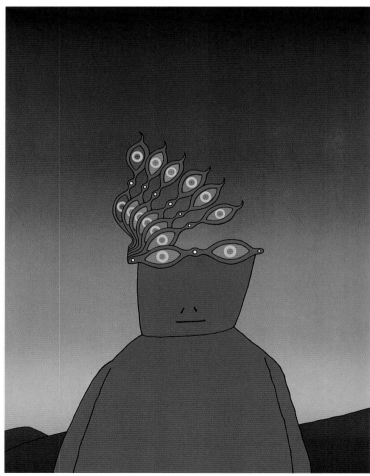

13 "Alice Editions" 「アリスエディションズ」1974

14 "Audio-visual" 「オーディオビジュアル」1971

15 "I Write You from a Distant Country" 「遠い異国より手紙を書く」1972

16 "The Art of Conversation" 「会話の芸術」1972

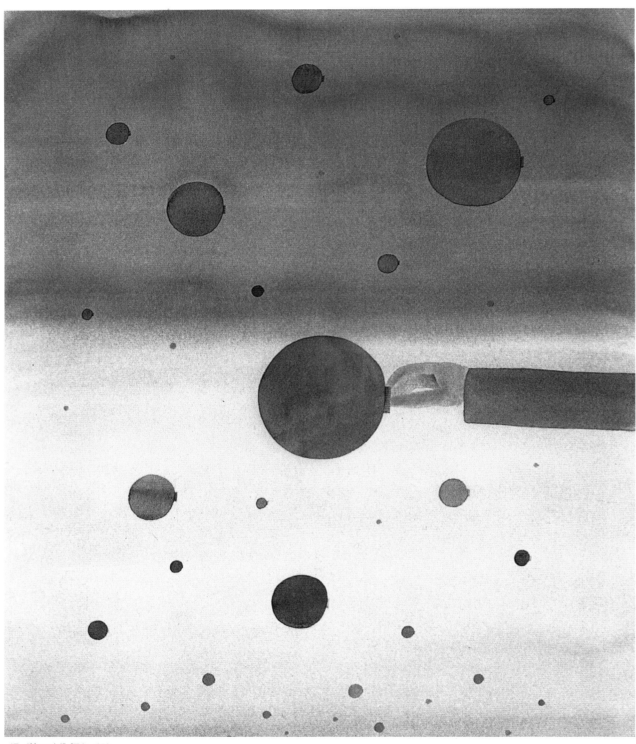

17 "Memorial" 「記念」1972

18　"Thinker"「考える人」1969

19　"Human Objet"「人間オブジェ」1967

Kafuka's Metamorphosis

20

Franz Kafka was both expressionist poet and novelist. *Metamorphosis* is one of his representative works. It tells the story of an ordinary salesman who awakens one morning to discover that he has been transformed into an insect with a hard carapace and numerous legs. In 1973 this nihilistic theme was taken up by Olivetti of Italy and a magnificent book was produced under Giorgio Soavi's direction—with illustrations by Jean-Michel Folon.

Folon portrays Kafka's insect beautifully, with pathos and humor. In my estimation it represents Folon's art at its very best.

フランツ・カフカは表現主義の詩人であり小説家である。小説『変身』は、彼の代表作である。平凡なセールスマンが、ある朝、自分が堅い殻と数本の足を持った昆虫に変身していることに気付く。このニヒリスティックなテーマを、1973年にジョルジオ・ソアベの企画でイタリアのオリベッティ社が取り上げ、フォロンのイラストレーションをつけて見事な本にした。

フォロンはカフカの昆虫を、悲しさとユーモアとで美しく表現している。恐らく、フォロン芸術の頂点を示す傑作だと思う。

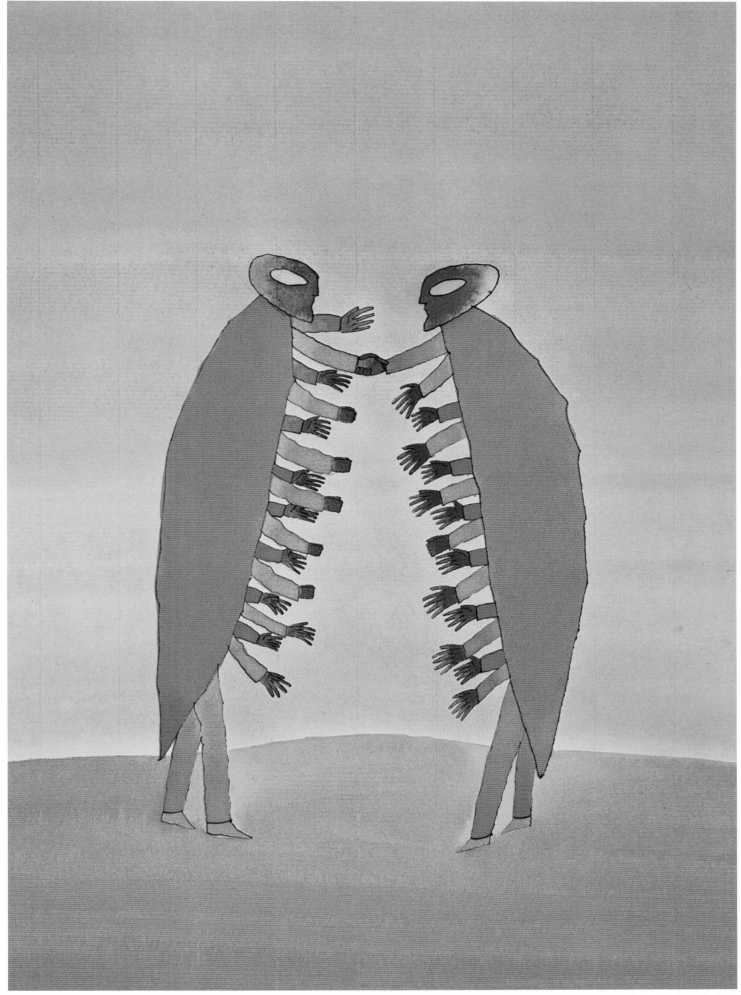

20-30 "Metamorphosis" 「変身」1973

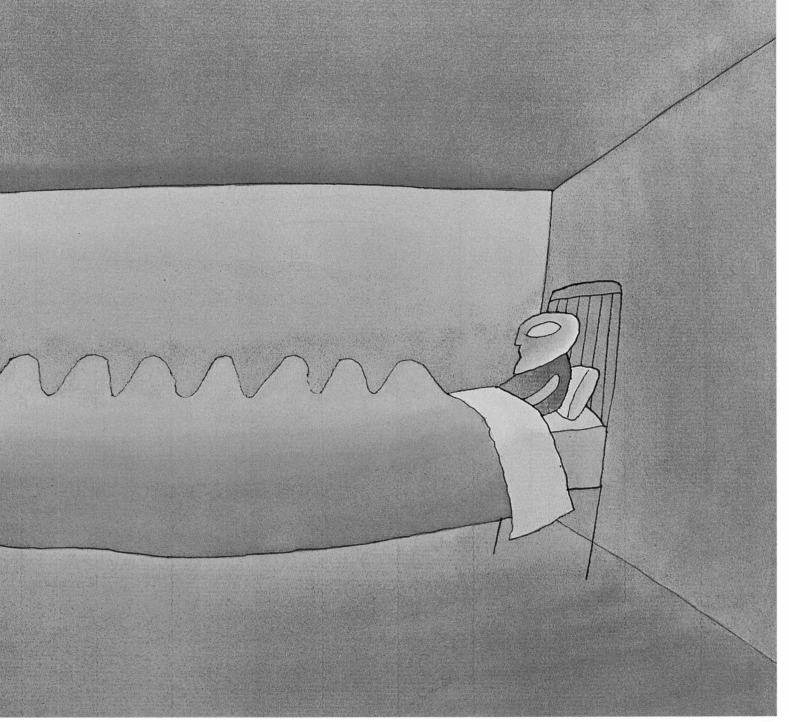

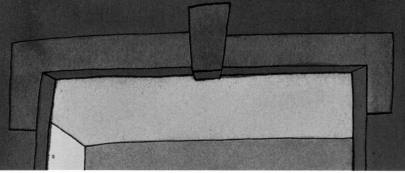

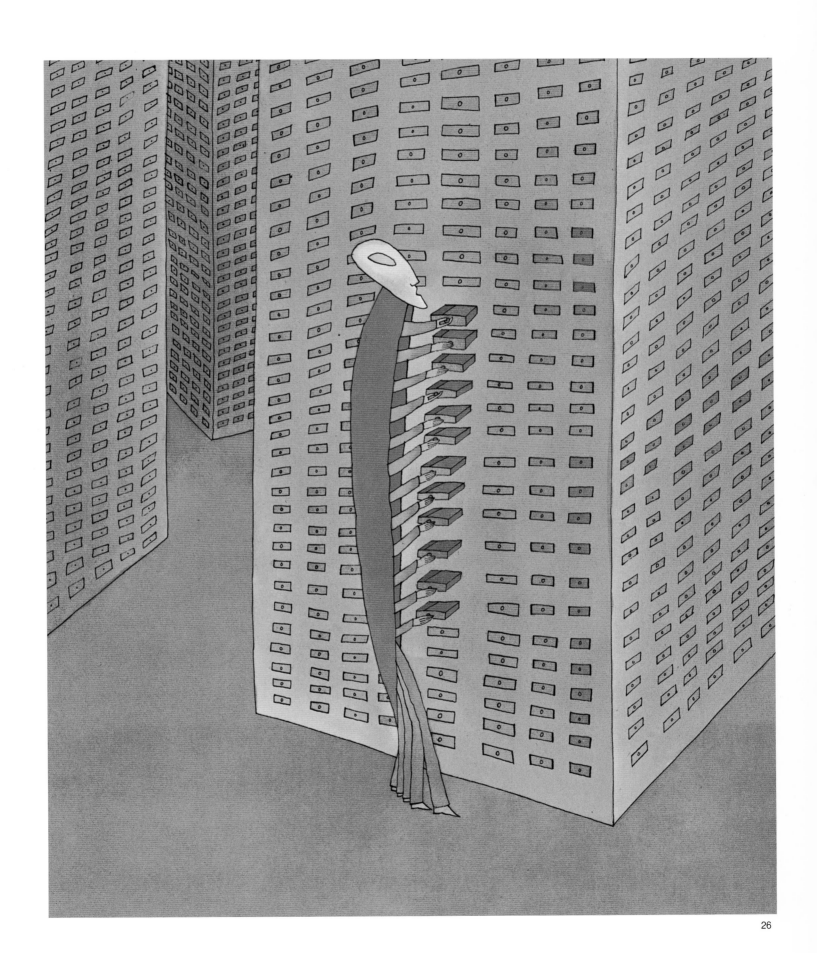

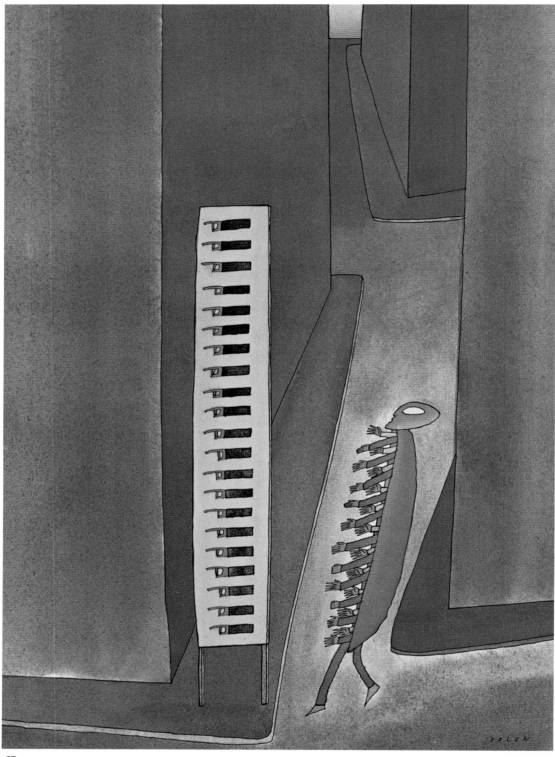

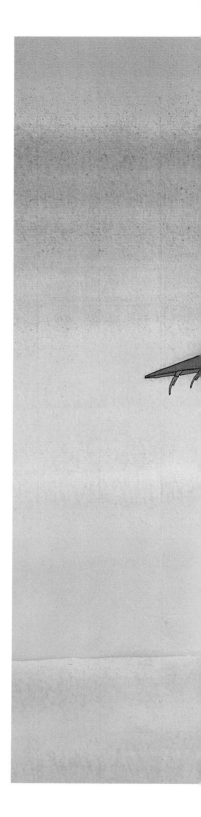

Kafuka's Metamorphosis

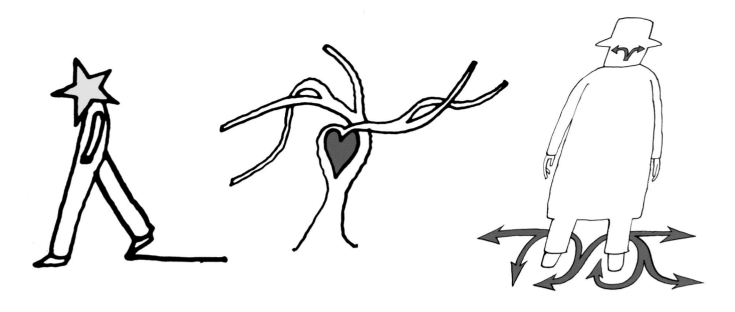

Daytime Dreamer さめた、夢見人

Hiroshi Kojitani 麹谷 宏

Meeting Jean-Michel Folon for the first time was an experience as unforgettable as it was surprising. With his air of fragile gentility and quiet profundity, he astonished me with his uncanny similarities to the aura created by his own succinct, philosophical artworks.

One should not be fooled by appearances, however. For Folon, despite his placid expression and gentle manner, possesses an almost unimaginably intense commitment to social and cultural values. Through his illustrations he speaks out broadly on issues such as human happiness, man's relationship with Nature, or even the spirituality of contemporary society.

At this point the reader might well assume that Folon's methods must be stuffy if not argumentative—yet this could not be farther from the truth. For Folon is neither a social critic nor a self-seeking idealist. He is merely a living being who is filled with sincere concern for the human community. Furthermore, to come in touch with his views not only arouses our empathy but instills equally strong convictions in us as well.

Many who set eyes on Folon's works are catatonically suspended in awe of them, not knowing how to respond to the questions which they seem to ask. Folon himself would surely revel to see such perplexed reactions, too. For on many occasions he has said that his foremost hope is that his illustrations might inspire their viewers to discover in them the images of themselves.

Folon may be likened to a philosopher-thinker with an artist's brush. Yet he does more than just philosophize and think. He also acts. In recent years, for example, he has become highly active in speaking out on social issues through volunteer work for Amnesty International and other organizations of this kind. As an example, when I asked to meet him while I was in Paris, he suggested that we rendezvous at Fouquet's, the famed cafe-restaurant on the Champs Elysées that has appeared in numerous works of literature and film. In recent years, however, Fouquet's became a focus of preservationist protest after this Parisian landmark was slated to be razed and replaced by a fast-food restaurant. Folon and his co-

フォロンに会って、おどろき、とまどってしまった。というのは、たよりないほどの優しさと、深い静けさをともなった彼の視線の表情が、簡潔で哲学的な空間のフォロンの絵が持つ情感と、あまりにも似かよっていたからである。

現代をただあわただしく生きる者は、深く素直な静けさに弱いのだ。そういえば、フォロンの絵をみる人が時々みせるあの考えこむような表情も、彼の絵の語りかけに、一瞬とまどってしまうからではないのだろうか。でも、もしフォロンがこういう場面をみたら、きっと喜ぶにちがいないと思う。フォロンはよく、「私の絵に誘われて、見る人が自分のイメージを拡げていってくれることこそ本望」と語っているからである。

しかし、人の見かけにだまされてはいけない。フォロンの、その静かな表情や語り方からはとても信じられないほどに、社会や文化に寄せる彼の思いは激しく、熱い。フォロンの話は、自分の絵を語りながら人間の幸せや自然との関わりといったことに拡がり、現代社会の精神性といった問題に延びてゆく。こう書くといかにも固苦しい議論っぽいが、フォロンの話は決して一人よがりの理想論でも社会批判でもなく、人間とその社会に向ける優しい思いに満ちあふれたもので、聞いているうちに共感する気持ちが次第に高まり、こちらの身体も熱くなってくる。

フォロンは、絵筆を持った思想家なのだ。そして思索するだけではなく、最近の彼の時間の多くはアムネスティ・インターナショナル（良心の囚人）など、いくつかの社会問題に関するボランティア活動に捧げられてもいるのである。ぼくたちのランデヴーにフォロンが指定した場所は、シャンゼリゼのカフェ「フーケ」だったが、ここも最近そんな活動の焦点になったところだったらしい。「フーケ」といえば、レマルクの「凱旋門」やヘミングウェイの「日はまた昇る」など数々の文学や映画に登場する有名なカフェ・レストランだが、ここが大資本に買いとられて何とファーストフードのレストランに変ろうとしていたところを、フォロンたちが立ちあがって世論を喚起し、このフランス文化のシンボルのような店を救ったのだという。

ジャン＝ミッシェル・フォロンは、1934年にベルギーのブリュッセルに生れた。

31-36　Illustrations　イラストレーション　1988-1989

activists collected their forces and raised a public outcry against this impending travesty, and eventually succeeded in rescuing one of France's cultural symbols from the wrecking ball.

Folon was born in Brussels, Belgium in 1934. From early childhood, he says, he spent his every day drawing pictures and dreaming of leading his life as an artist. After reaching adulthood he veered slightly in direction and elected to study architecture at a well-known school. But his aspirations as an artist eventually proved too strong to ignore. He thus resolved to move to Paris and set himself up as a graphic artist.

During the next four years he experienced what was to become a highly formative phase of his life. Not only did his stay in Paris raise his concern over society's adulation of materialism and technology—issues he would subsequently address in his illustration work—it also provided him with his source of artistic inspiration as manifested in his famed use of arrows, traffic signs and concrete mazes.

Folon's works invariably rely on these motifs to portray the desolate void he detects in the 20th century. Nevertheless his illustrations always reveal the underlying warmheartedness of their creator. For above all Folon's works are poetic paeans sung in praise of the human spirit. That Folon and his works are deeply loved and admired by the citizens of France is nowhere more clearly demonstrated than in the selection of his design to serve as the official symbol of the French Bicentennial.

What attracts me so strongly to Folon's works is not so much their interest as "art" as their achievement in "creativity." It has been said that all men become poets at least once during their lives. But Folon has possessed a poet's powers of observation and sensitivity throughout his life. His illustrations always tell a story— a story of dreams. One thus does not *view* a Folon artwork—one *reads* it. It is for this reason that Folon has been called a "creator of dreams," and he himself on occasion has referred to himself as a "daytime dreamer"—one who dares to dream in real life.

もの心ついたときからもう毎日絵を描いていて、自分はこうして絵とともに一生をおくるのだと信じて疑わなかったそうだ。その後、ヴァン・ド・ヴェルドが創立した有名な学校で建築を学ぶが、やはり絵をすてきれず、グラフィックアーチストとして身を立てるためにパリに出る。しかしこの4年間は、後のフォロンの創作主題となる物質文明、技術文明に対する意識を持ち、また有名なキャラクターとなった矢印や交通標識、コンクリートの迷路などという表現の発想源を得たという意味で、実に貴重な体験であった。

フォロンの絵が語られるときには、決ってこれらのモチーフによる20世紀の荒涼たる心象風景という解説がつくのだが、しかしよくみれば、その絵の中には作家の暖かい心がみえるはずだ。フォロンの絵は、究極、人間讃歌の詩画にほかならない。

ぼくは、フォロンの絵をみるとき、artという概念よりもcreativityという姿勢に、より強くひきつけられる。人間は誰しも生涯に一度は詩人であるといわれるが、フォロンはずっと、詩人の洞察力と感性を持ち続けて、絵の中に夢の物語を語り続けてきた作家なのだ。だから、人はフォロンの絵をみるのではなく、フォロンの夢の物語を読んでその絵に心を寄せるのではないのだろうか。「夢の配達人」と評されるゆえんだろう。フランス革命200周年の公式シンボルにフォロンのデザインが選ばれたのも、フォロンの心がフランスの人々に深く愛され支持されていることの何よりの証拠ではないだろうか。

フォロンは自分のことを、「さめた、夢見人」(rêve réveillée)といっている。美しくやさしい言葉だが、フォロンはこの言葉になみなみならぬ自負の思いを込めているような気がしてならない。そして、かつてフォロンのことを、「絵を描くモラリスト」(pantre moralist)と好評していた勝見勝が生きていてこの言葉を聞いたら、きっと、「フォロンは相変らず若いな」と喜んだにちがいないと思った。

37 "Metropolis"「大都会」1978

38 "Lifeless"「命を失って」1979

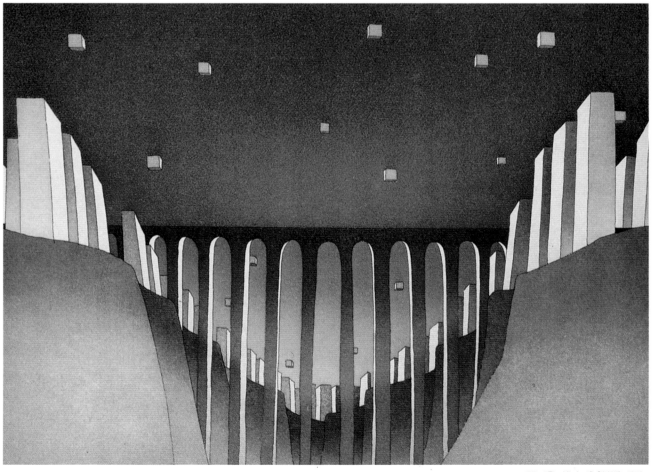

39 "The Viaduct"「高架橋」1979

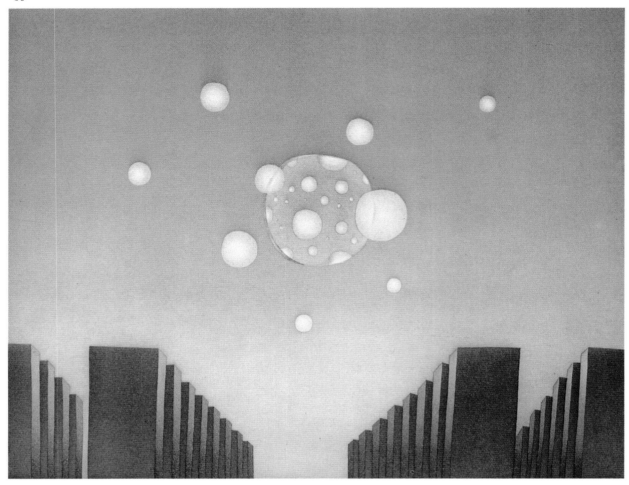

40 "Opening"「入口」1979

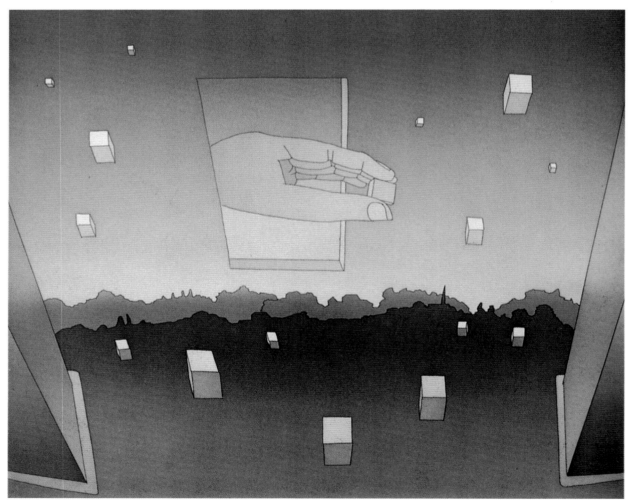

41 "Tomorrow"「明日」1980

42　"The Man Who Planted Trees"「木を植えた男」1982

43　"Alone"「ひとり」1979

44 "Piazza" 「広場」1980

45

45-49 "Over the Rainbow" 「虹のかなた」 1980-1981

48

50 "Crowd"「群衆」1979

51 "Secret" 「秘密」 1979

52 "Spring" 「春」1989

53 "Dialogue" 「対話」1980

54-58 "Universal Declaration of Human Rights" 「世界人権宣言」1988

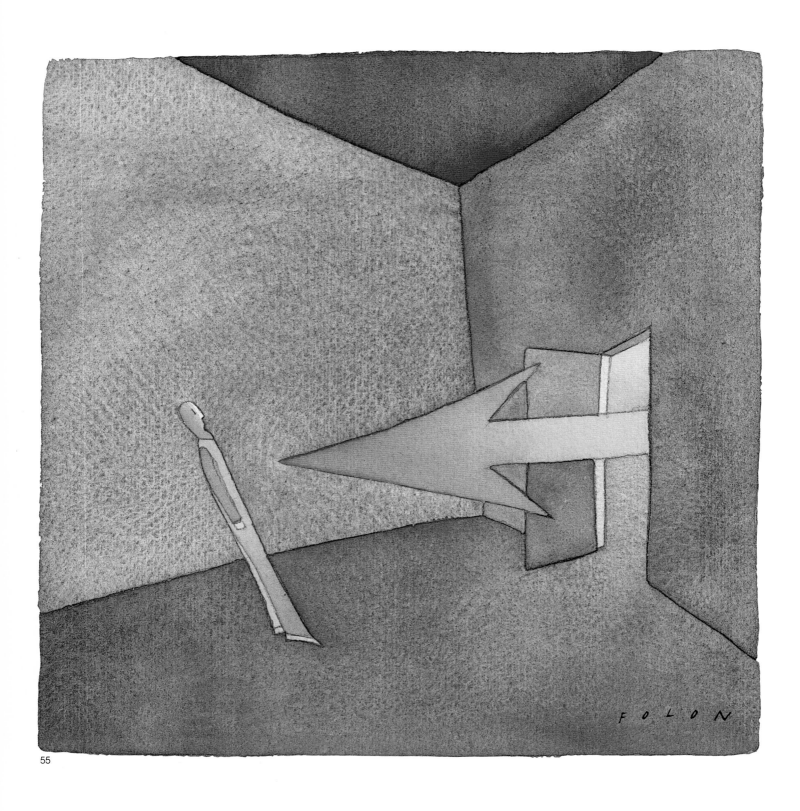

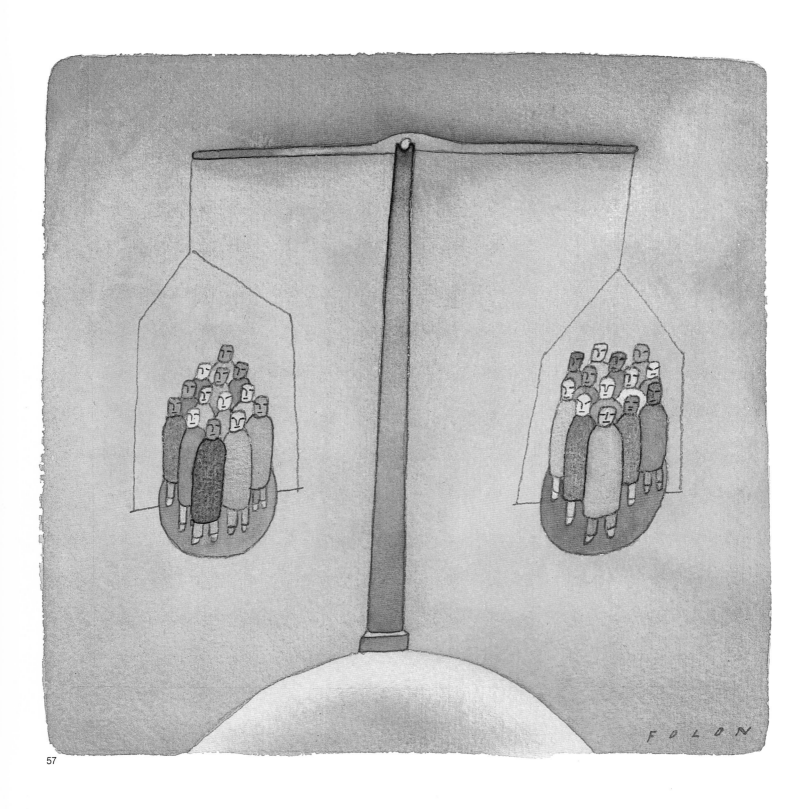

58

59 "City"「都会」1988

60

60-66 Illustrations for management consulting firm 経営コンサルティング会社のためのイラスト 1989

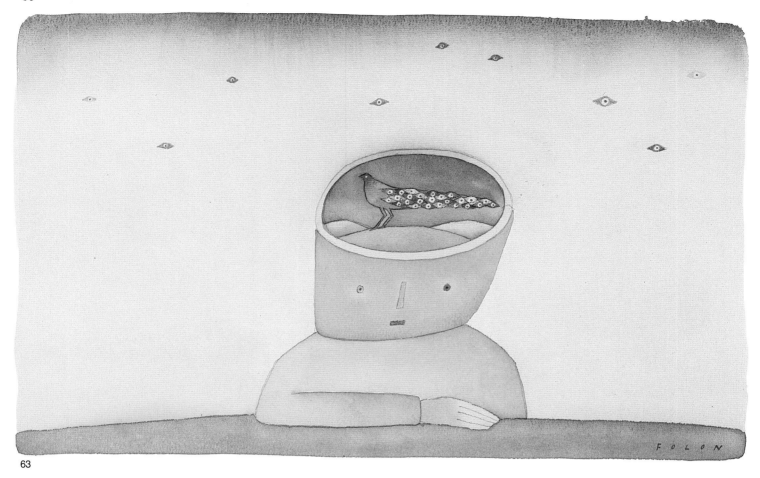

63

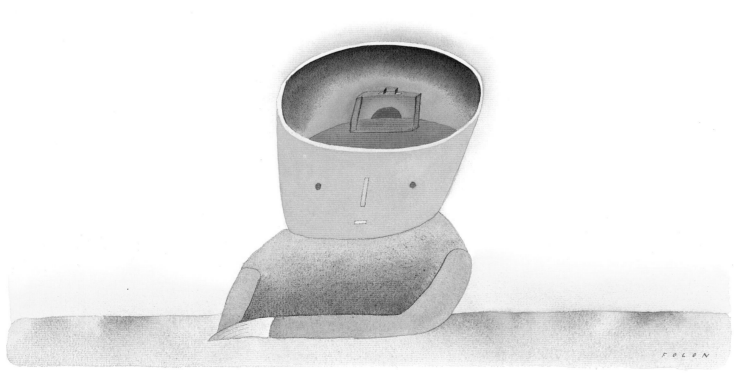

65

67 Illustration for golf club ゴルフクラブのためのイラスト 1989

68 Illustration for travel agency 旅行代理店のためのイラスト 1989

70-71　Illustrations for gift promotion campaign of department store　百貨店ギフトセールのためのイラスト　1989

72-73 Illustrations for gift promotion campaign of department store 百貨店ギフトセールのためのイラスト 1988

KATSURA FUNAKOSHI 舟越 桂 Sculptor

Tadayasu Sakai 酒井忠康

There I was, enjoying a quiet breakfast with a friend at an outdoor cafe in San Marco Square, having come to Venice for the 1988 biennale, when David Sylvester, the British art critic, suddenly came along and tapped me on the shoulder.

"Katsura Funakoshi even outdoes John Davies," he asserted with a smile on his face. Whereupon he gave me a thumbs-up sign and proceeded on his way.

John Davies is a British sculptor who had caught my attention for some time. He is an oddity even among his compatriots in his field, and his works, which portray the human condition in disturbingly real terms, are somewhat horrifying.

Sylvester's intention, it seemed to me, was not to say that Katsura Funakoshi was a better sculptor than John Davies. He was merely using Davies for purposes of comparison to convey just how high his respect for Funakoshi was. In retrospect, however, Sylvester also appeared to be telling me not to be too disappointed. You see, despite Sylvester's enthusiastic praise, Funakoshi failed to receive a prize at the biennale. Sylvester was one of the judges.

The reason why this episode remains so firmly imprinted in my memory is related to my great surprise at seeing young Funakoshi receive so much attention at what was his first international showing. Actually, I should have been the *last* person to be so surprised, considering it was I who had commissioned his participation in the first place.

It is difficult to explain precisely what makes Funakoshi's works so alluring. Part of their appeal, I imagine, lies in their lifelike detail, a trait that negates the necessity for stuffy explanations of the kind we have gotten used to in treating contemporary art. Funakoshi's works also seem to cast a sympathetic gaze on mankind, one which the rest of us have somehow lost along the way. Technically, his works borrow from Gothic and Buddhist sculpture, and yet they manifest no recognizable traces of such fusions. His sculptures are magnificently creative, but not in any way pretentious.

Funakoshi knows quite well that his greatest strength lies in his own natural sensitivity. He creates not from the mind but from the heart. His portrait sculptures, for example, do not depict real persons but persons Funakoshi would wish to know. With a skillfully molded eyeline he transforms what would normally be an expressionless face into a "living" soul. For example in "Afternoon in Gunter Grove," which was Funakoshi's first attempt at full-length sculpture, the figure appears to be leaning forward as if on the verge of taking a step.

Funakoshi's works are so exquisitely detailed that you can almost hear his chisel at work. They are carved in camphor wood and lightly painted, creating a colorful yet translucent image seeming to emerge straight out of a painting. With their piercing marble eyes, they are so true to life that you are tempted to reach out and touch them to confirm your suspicions. Yet at the same time they also arouse inexplicable feelings of nostalgia—the nostalgia of reuniting with a long-lost friend.

それは1988年のヴェネツィア・ビエンナーレでのことである。たまたまサン・マルコ広場のカフェ・テラスで友人と朝食をとっていたところへイギリスの美術評論家ディビット・シルヴェスターがやってきて、開口一番こんなことを言った。〝ジョーン・ディビーズよりも舟越桂のほうがドライである〟と。そして親指を立てて、わたしの肩をポンとたたいた。

ディビーズというのは、まえから気になっていたイギリスの作家である。その作品はいささかおどろおどろしいところがあって、人間の実存的な情況を具象化し、イギリスの彫刻界でも異色の存在である。シルヴェスターの指摘はもちろん、どちらが上質だ、ということではない。比較の妙として、なるほどとおもわせるのである。しかし、シルヴェスターの賛意をえた舟越ではあったが、残念ながら賞からはずれた。親指を立てて、わたしの肩をポンとたたいたのは、気にするな、という彼の親切だと、いまはおもっている。シルヴェスターはビエンナーレの賞の審査員の一人だった。

こんなことをおもいだしたのも、舟越桂という若い日本の彫刻家が、はじめて国際的な舞台にその作品を出品し、大いに注目されたという事実に、コミッショナーであるわたしさえ驚いてしまったからなのである。

魅力の根源を説明するのはむずかしいが、ひとつだけ言えるのは、肖像彫刻に類する作品のせいだろうとおもう。現代美術に久しくつきまとってきた、いささか堅苦しい説明を必要としない。わたしたちが、どこかに置き忘れてきた人間にたいする、ある感応的なまなざしを感じさせる。技法的にもゴシック彫刻や日本の仏像彫刻からさまざまな要素をかりてきていながら、舟越の作品には、そうしたものの引用の継目がみあたらない。なにかあっけらかんとしていて、すぐれて独創的なのである。

別のことばで言えば、自分になにが可能であるか、ということをよく知っているということである。それは〝フィーリング〟を大事にするということ。そして考えのための考えから作品をつくるのではなく、自分のなかの〝時の想い〟をかたちにする。だから特定の人物の場合もあるが、こんなふうな人と出会えたらいいな、とひそかに念じているような人物の作品もある。左右にわずかに開いた目線は、身ぶり同様、表情を固定したものから動きのあるものに変える一瞬であるし、たとえば、「午後にはガンター・グローヴにいる」のような、はじめて試みられた全身像の場合には、わずかに前のめりになっている。

いろいろ細かい神経をつかってつくられているその作品は、着色されていて絵からぬけだしたようなところがあるが、半透明にすける木の色味が触覚を刺激する。作品に近づいて、ふと触ってみたくなるのはそのせいかもしれない。ノミの音がきこえてくるのである。しばらく眺めているうちに、ある懐かしさの感情が湧いてくる。〝時の想い〟につれだされるからである。

しかし、どこかで会ったことのある人物だ、という確認はできない。なぜなら舟越は、自分のなかの〝彫刻〟を刻んでいるからである。

1 "Between Words and Woods" 「言葉と森の間に立って」 1989 P：佐藤時啓

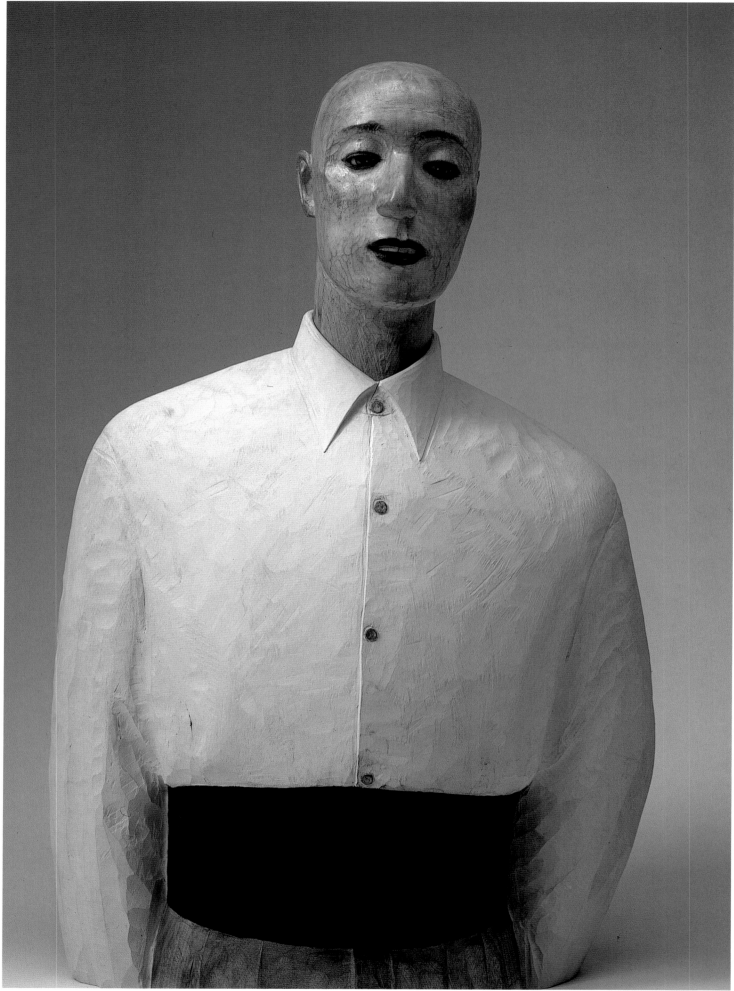

2 "Oblique Clouds" 「傾いた雲」 1988

3 "Gentle Head Wind"「静かな向かい風」1988

4　"Saving up Wind"「風をためて」1983

5 "Like a Stack of Half-read Books" 「積んである読みかけの本のように」1983

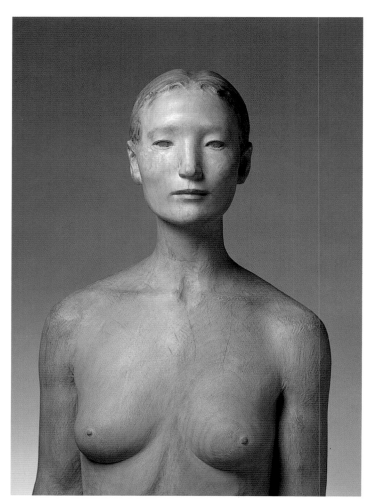

6 "Portrait of Mr. Nakano" 「中野の肖像」1988

7 "Portrait of My Wife" 「妻の肖像」1981

8 "White Song" 「白い歌をきいた」1984

9 "Thirst and Speed" 「渇きとスピード」1988

10 "Man in a Suit" 「背広の男」1982

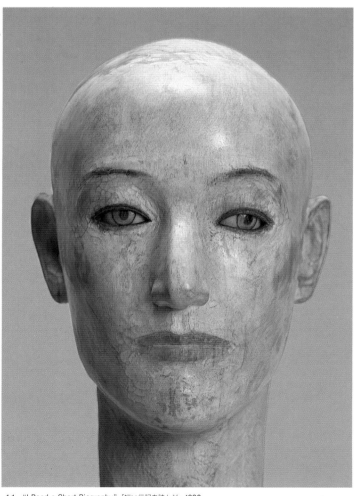

11 "I Read a Short Biography" 「短い伝記を読んだ」1986

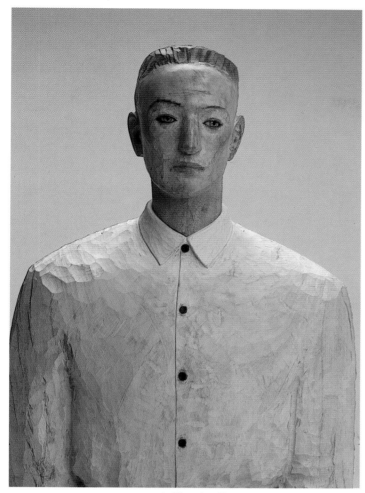

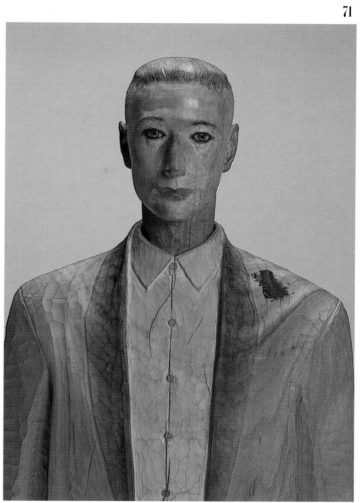

12　"Memories of Ramses"「ラムセスにまつわる記憶」1986

13　"Water Drops"「消えない水滴」1985

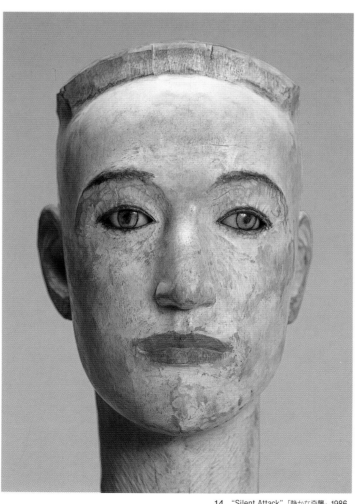

14　"Silent Attack"「静かな奇襲」1986

15 "Church and Café" 「教会とカフェ」 1988

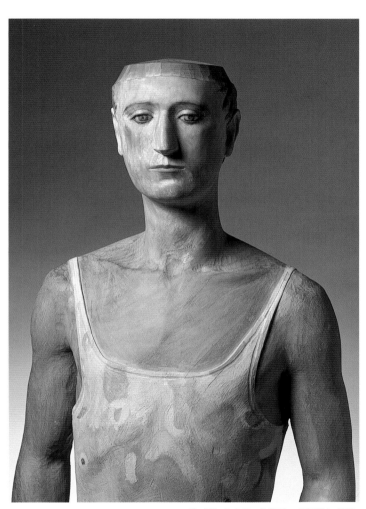

16　"Why Rudy Runs"「ルディーの走る理由」1982　　　　　　　　　　　　　　17　"Etude"「会議のための習作」1980

18 "Winter Book" 「冬の本」1988

19 "Sand and City" 「砂と街と」 1986

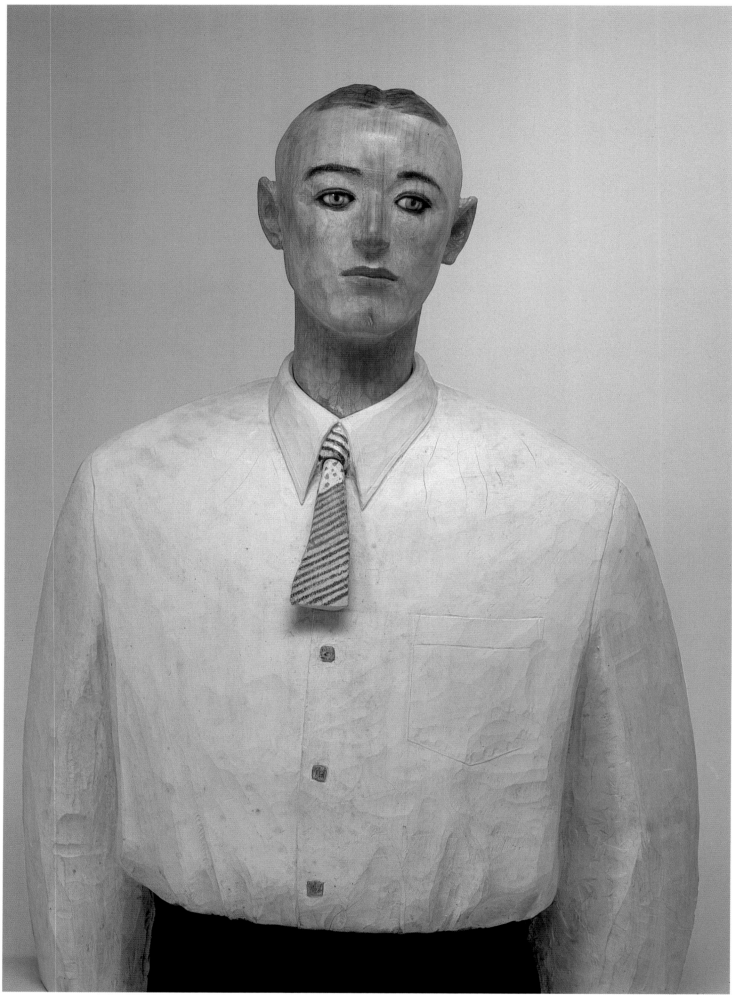

20 "Long Monologue" 「長い独り言」1988

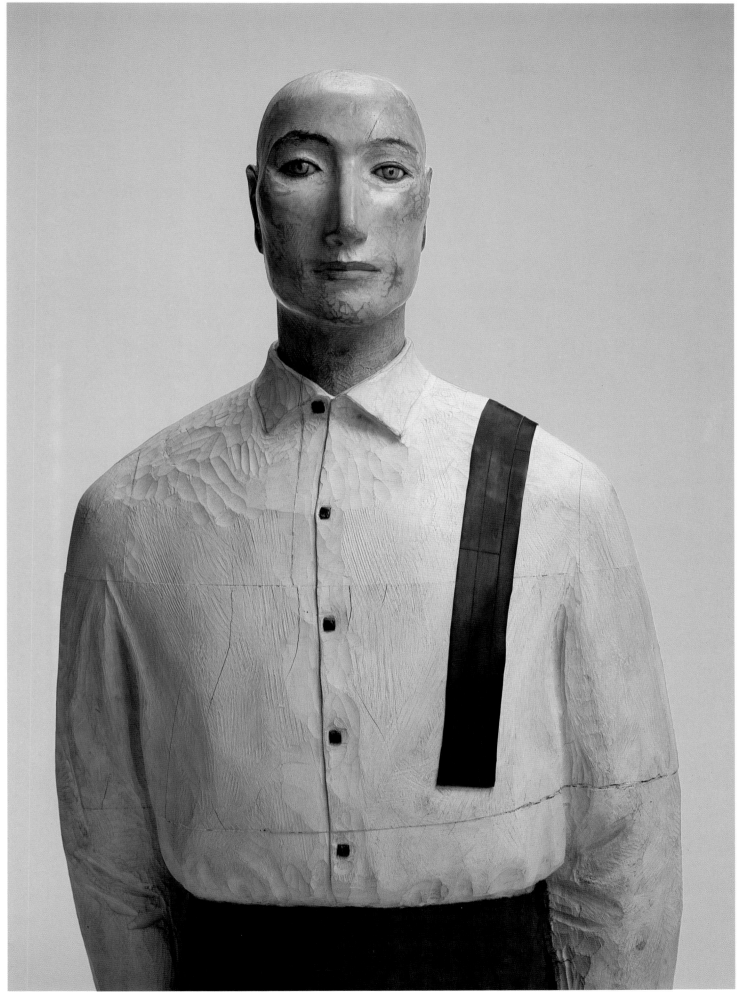

21 "Trip to the Woods" 「森へ行く日」 1984

Grand Master Series 巨匠シリーズ—4
OTL AICHER オトル・アイヒャー

Shutaro Mukai 向井周太郎

The name Otl Aicher immediately calls to mind a number of associations. Initiator of the post-war design movement espoused by the Design School of Ulm. Influential advocate of visual communication. Creator of Lufthansa's corporate identity system. Director of graphic design for the 1972 Munich Olympics and inventor of the innovative pictogram system introduced there. Chief planner of signs at Frankfurt and Munich Airports. And on and on.

Among his many accomplishments to date perhaps the most noteworthy is Aicher's system of pictograms designed in conjunction with the Munich Olympics. It consists of pictographic symbols for each event which are based on a unified grid system, much in the manner of a typeface system. As this approach suggests, Aicher's designs are always based on a methodology that embraces elements both of functional practicality and rationalism; yet at the same time they are invariably imbued with a supremely appealing "humane" warmth that transcends theoretics.

Aicher is also an outstanding photographer. As his aerial photos of Germany and other areas of Europe shot for Lufthansa demonstrate—or his collections of photos of the Sahara Desert—Aicher exudes a profound love of nature and the environment, combined with sensitive powers of observation. These traits give his photographic works lofty status as rare achievements of historical import.

After the Munich Olympics Aicher shifted his base of operations to the highlands of southern Germany, close to the Alps. Since then he has dedicated his time chiefly to design research and design projects of a controversial nature, consistently probing how to reach a harmonious balance between man and his natural environment.

One of Aicher's more recent controversial design projects is his collection of illustrations prepared for the biography of the 14th C. philosopher Wilhelm von Ockham. Like his earlier projects—such as his provocative critiques of kitchen architecture or the automobile—in this collection of illustrations Aicher aims to stir controversy through his design media. In von Ockham Aicher seems to have discovered an early proponent who shared his persistent espousal of freedom and his staunch faith in actions rather than abstractions. Through this project Aicher succeeded in arousing renewed interest in this philosopher of the Middle Ages.

I was fortunate to have the opportunity to visit Aicher as he was working on these von Ockham illustrations. I was amazed to rediscover his rich conceptual powers and beauty of line, particularly considering that he had extremely limited visual reference materials to work from owing to the antiquity of von Ockham's era. Aicher's aim here is to depart from modern constructivism and to reestablish a new realm of representationalism. He adopts the parallel perspective and multi-focal layout characteristic of ancient Japanese picture scrolls which, combined with a unique four-layer picture division, produce a wholly new artistic effect. One might call them contemporary picture scrolls. They feature a superb polyphony of colors—bright, sanguine colors that Aicher seems to extract from the natural beauty of his Bavarian surroundings.

オトル・アイヒャーといえば、ウルム造形大学による第2次大戦後のデザイン運動の推進者として、あるいはビジュアル・コミュニケーションの提唱者として、ドイツ・ルフトハンザ航空のCI、ミュンヘン・オリンピックの総合ディレクションとピクトグラムの展開、フランクフルトおよびミュンヘン空港の総合サイン計画などの先駆的な成果がまず想起されるだろう。

なかでも、ミュンヘン・オリンピックにおいて一貫したグリッド・システムから展開された競技種目のピクトグラムは、一つのタイプフェイスのような統一的シンボルとしてサイン・デザインの画期的な模範例となった。そのアプローチが端的に示すように、アイヒャーのデザイン展開はいつも機能性と理性的な方法意識に貫かれているが、その造形の特質はつねに理論をこえて人間性豊かな詩が香り実に魅力的だ。しかしまたアイヒャーの写真家としての仕事もすばらしい。ルフトハンザのためのドイツやヨーロッパ大陸の航空写真をはじめサハラ砂漠の写真集などは、彼の風土や環境に対する深い愛情と人間的洞察のまなざしが捉えた貴重な歴史的作品である。

ミュンヘン・オリンピックの後は、アイヒャーはアルプスに近い南独の高原ローティスにデザイン活動の場を移し、自然と人間文化の共生の在り方を探りながら、もっぱらデザイン研究と問題提起のためのデザイン・プロジェクトに取り組んでいる。

先般ggg（ギンザ・グラフィック・ギャラリー）で一部が紹介された『哲学者・フォン・オッカム伝』のイラストレーションの仕事もその一つである。地域文化の観点から台所を捉え直した『調理のためのキッチン——近代建築的な教義の終焉』や自動車100年の形態変遷史を描出した『自動車批評』などに次ぐ、書物あるいはポスターというメディアを通じての問題提起のデザインであり、哲学者や美術史家の協力を得て、中世の哲学者オッカム・ルネッサンスの契機をもたらしたものだ。オッカムの思想のうちに、アイヒャーがたえず主張する自由と、抽象的な観念よりも具体的な行為のなかに真実を見る具体の哲学の先駆性を発見していたからである。

アイヒャーがちょうどこのスケッチに取り組んでいたとき、私は別のプロジェクトの協力でその場に立ち会う機会に恵まれたが、オッカムの肖像画もその生涯の視覚的資料もない時代の、きわめて乏しい周辺資料から描出していくアイヒャーの構想力の豊かさと線描の美しさには、あらためて驚かされた。ここでは、西欧近代の抽象的な構成主義からの離陸、いかに新しい次元で具象を再建するかという試みもテーマである。また画面構成には、日本の絵巻にみられる平行透視と図の多焦点的配置がとりこまれ、ユニークな4層の画面分割とからめて物語の時空間作用の新しい形式が生みだされている。まさに新しい絵巻だ。

この色彩のポリフォニーも実に美しい。ミュンヘン・オリンピックがバイエルンの自然や風物の色を表象し、明るく爽やかな色彩の祭典であったように、アイヒャーの色彩はたえず自然から汲みあげられているように思われる。なお近作のコンピュータ・フォントのためのタイプフェイス4種も間もなく国際的に共有化されていくだろう。

"Wilhelm von Ockham-The Risk of Modern Thought" 『ヴィルヘルム・フォン・オッカム—現代哲学の先駆者』1986

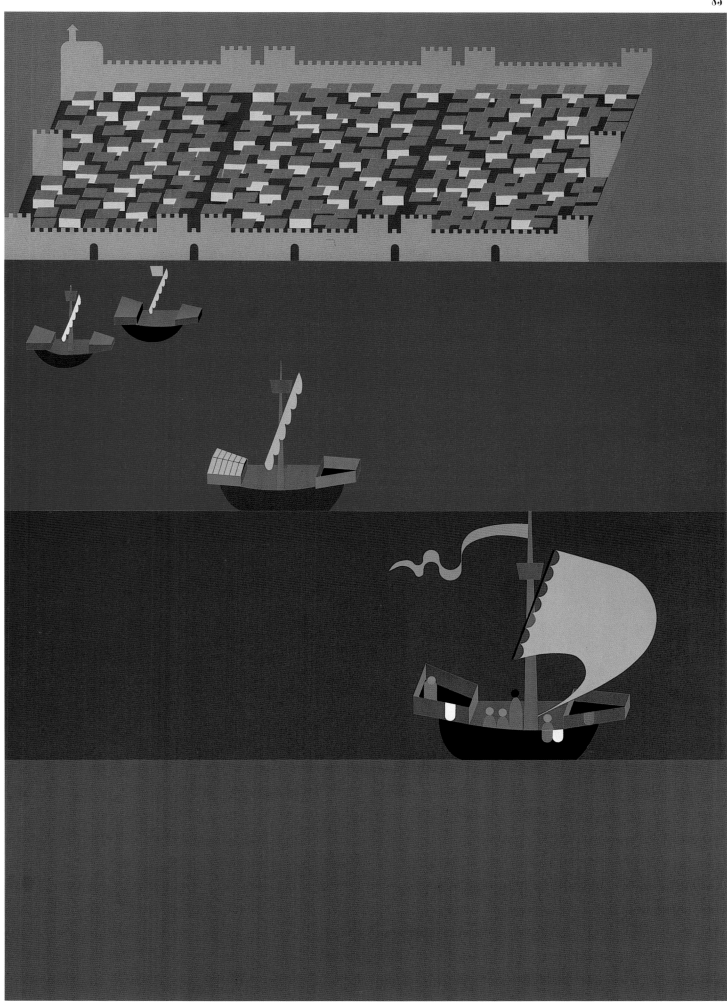

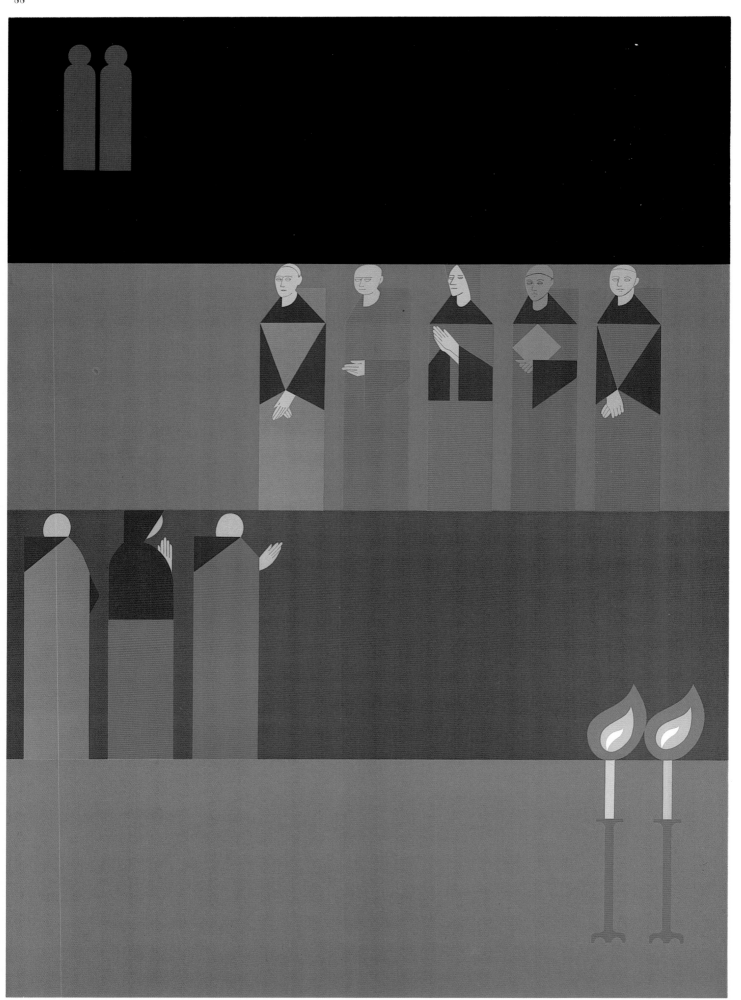

NORIKO UENO 上野紀子

Yoshiaki Tono　東野芳明

I first learned of Noriko Ueno quite a long time ago, through the late Shuzo Takiguchi. He introduced me to one of her works, a heartwarming book for children that she had produced in collaboration with her husband, Yoshio Nakae. If memory serves me right, it was entitled *Microcosm*.

It was the story of a strabismic young girl named Chico. I found myself greatly attracted to the book in part, perhaps, because Chico bore a resemblance to my own daughter, who was then about four or five. Ueno had provided the artwork; her husband, the beautifully poetic text. The story was based on the premise of a girl who always looks at the world with one eye through a telescope. For those of us with normal sight, it aimed to depict a flowing stream of unusual images, a fantasy world of endless wonder.

Shuzo Takiguchi was an avid admirer of Lewis Carroll's Alice-in-Wonderland stories, and in Noriko Ueno's Chico character he seems to have found a second Alice. Chico, who never for a moment set her telescope aside, was like a younger version of Alice in the land behind the mirror. In fact some have even suggested that Carroll's title *Through the Looking Glass* could conceivably be read to mean "through a telescope."

Ueno once drew a large portrait of Shuzo Takiguchi. To understand it requires a certain amount of explanation, however. There is an extant photograph of Takiguchi which shows him "peeking" into "Etant Donnés," a painting by Marcel Duchamp that hangs in the Philadelphia Museum of Fine Art. The painting depicts a completely empty room except for an old wooden door in one wall; peering through the keyhole reveals a woman lying naked, her legs spread apart, one hand holding a gas lamp. It is a strange panorama painted by Duchamp in his final years.

In the aforementioned photo of Takiguchi, one sees only the old wooden door and Takiguchi's back view. What Ueno did was to transfer the photograph onto a large canvas, applying the photo-realism technique which was then in vogue in the art world. In the resulting portrait of an old surrealist poet peering at a strange world through a keyhole, it is conceivable that Ueno sought to overlap Takiguchi's image with that of Chico and her fascination with her telescope.

In 1981 Ueno published a truly unusual children's book entitled *Journey to the Stars*. In this work Chico's telescope remains attached to her eye, focusing in on objects at will and enabling her to travel through space at the "speed of thought," which is even faster than the speed of light. In this work too, a poetic and unconventional realm of time and space fills every page. Yet the effect is not forced but quite natural, much like the world of Duchamp.

Duchamp himself had great interest in the extrasensory world. For example, he suggested that our three-dimensional realm actually contains an invisible fourth dimension. He also wrote about seeing things with one eye and hearing things with one ear. Is this not the world of Chico too? And Chico, who "sees" beyond the realm of three dimensions into a fourth dimension—is her single eye not like the vision of Duchamp?

上野紀子のことを知ったのは、ずい分前、故瀧口修造を通してだった。ご主人の中江嘉男との共作絵本を見せられて、ほのぼのとした憶えがある。たしか『小宇宙』という本では、やぶにらみのチコという少女の顔が当時4、5歳だったわが娘に似ていたせいもあって、大へん魅力的だった。そこにはご主人のきわめて詩的テキストがそえられ、ぼくらが2つの眼で見ている日常世界を、望遠鏡で片目だけで見るという設定を通して、非日常の幻想の世界が泉のように静かに湧きあがっていた。

あるいはもう1冊の本は、長いひさしの円帽子をかぶったチコの顔と、たしかインドでの航空事故で奇跡的に助かった外国人の女の子の顔写真が見開きにあって、この本の中身のすべてが、この2つのイメージの繰返して出来上がっている、という奇抜でたのしい実験的な本だった。同じイメージが、分厚い本のヴォリュームの中でふくれあがり、自己増殖し、厚みのある物に化した、という感じである。

ルイス・キャロルのアリス物語を愛した瀧口修造は、上野紀子のチコのなかに、もうひとりのアリスを見ていたようだった。望遠鏡を手ばなさないチコは『鏡の国のアリス』の妹だったのかもしれない。そもそも、原題のThrough the Looking Glass は、読みようによっては「望遠鏡を通して」と読めないこともない、という説があるくらいなのだから。

その上野紀子が瀧口修造の大きな肖像画を描いたことがある。これには説明がいるだろう。瀧口さんがフィラデルフィア美術館にある、マルセル・デュシャンの「遺作」を覗きこんでいる写真がある。「遺作」とは、空っぽの部屋の壁に古い木の扉があって、その扉の穴から中を覗くと、女の裸像が股を開いて横たわり、手にガス灯のランプをかかげ持っているのが見えるという、最晩年の異様な覗きパノラマ作品である。瀧口の肖像写真には、その扉と彼の後姿しか写っていない。上野紀子は、当時美術界で話題になっていたフォト・レアリズムの手法に倣って、この写真を大きなカンヴァスにそっくり描きこんだのである。この場合、望遠鏡ならぬ扉の穴を覗いて、不思議な世界に見入っている老シュルレアリスト詩人の姿に、上野紀子は、望遠鏡を手ばなさないチコのイメージを重ね合わせた、といえなくもない。

1981年に出版された『宇宙遊星間旅行』という奇想天外な絵本は、チコの片眼に望遠鏡がくっついてしまい、勝手に焦点がのびていって、宇宙空間に達し、「ひとりの星」と出会って、光より速い「思考速」のことなどの話をするという、異次元物語である。ここにも、異次元という非日常空間時間の詩情が本のすみずみにあふれていて、こじつけではなく、デュシャン的世界にも思える。デュシャンもまた、日常では見えない領域に関心をもち、たとえば3次元世界は、不可視の4次元が可視の3次元に投影された世界だと考えついたのである。あるメモに「片目デ見ルコト、片耳デ聴クコト」とあるところなど、期せずして、片目のチコを思わせるではないか。

チコの片目は、3次元をこえて4次元を「見る」仕掛である点でも、じつにデュシャン的な眼ではあるまいか。

1 "Journey to the Stars"「宇宙遊星間飛行」1980

2-3 "Mirror Land" 「鏡の国」 1983

3

4 "With a Rose" 「薔薇と」 1976

5　"Journey to the Stars"「宇宙遊星間飛行」1980

6　"With a Rose"「薔薇と」1976

7　"Mirror Land"「鏡の国」1983

8 "Journey to the Stars"「宇宙遊星間飛行」1981

9 "Journey to the Stars"「宇宙遊星間飛行」1980

10 "Journey to the Stars" 「宇宙遊星間飛行」1981

11 "Journey to the Stars" 「宇宙遊星間飛行」 1981

12 "Journey to the Stars" 「宇宙遊星間飛行」 1980

13 "Journey to the Stars" 「宇宙遊星間飛行」 1981

14 "With Flowers" 「花たちと」 1976

15 "Door Land" 「扉の国」 1978

16

16-17 "Door Land" 「扉の国」1977

18 "Door Land" 「扉の国」1978

19 "Mirror Room" 「鏡の部屋」1973

20 "Balloon Room" 「気球の部屋」1972

21 "Chair Room" 「椅子の部屋」1973

22 "Wind Room" 「風の部屋」1973

23 "Door Land" 「扉の国」 1978

24 "Room of Flowers" 「花の部屋」1972

25 "Room of Birds" 「鳥の部屋」1973

26 "Boat Room" 「船の部屋」1972

27 "Eyelids" 「瞼の眼」1986

MIECZYSŁAW GÓROWSKI ミェチスワフ・グロフスキー

Raymond Vézina レイモン・ヴェジナ

The art of Mieczysław Górowski, manifested in over 230 posters, has come to be known all over the world for the originality of the psychological universe he has conceived. It is a universe of ochre, the color of earth, a color that the artist uses to stress his taste for fundamental things such as the earth itself.

The objects in his posters are all basic, simple objects of every-day life. He especially loves textures, and when he was a student of sculpture and painting he experimented with paper, wood, leather, fabric, even metal. The maquette of *The Police*, for example, was done directly on a rusted metal plate about 40 centimeters high.

Górowski developed his inborn taste for monumental forms in the Architecture Department of the Fine Arts Academy in Cracow. "When one day," he says, "the professor asked us to scale some pieces of wood placed on a big uniform surface, I increased all dimensions considerably without even realizing it." One can refer to *Encounter with Spanish Culture in Jelenia Gora* and *Towards the Light*.

His passions for ochre and its shades, for texture and for monu-mentality can be viewed as the raw material of his poster creations. He is constantly on the lookout for new, original ways of expressing the abundance of life, everyday hardships and sorrows of man caused by the doings of other men.

In the theater Górowski has found the kind of emotional energy that best suits the dynamic expressiveness of his concepts. In *Antigone*, the ropes that have cut through the body tying it to the ground introduce a new symbol for the tragic power of destiny. These ropes do much more than merely immobilize the body: they pierce through the limbs touching the spectator in whom the suffer-ing of the victim becomes his own emotion.

In Górowski's universe man occupies the central position. The artist tries to find a rare association that the fundamental concept will spring from. The tied-up face in *The Police* is a magnificent example of surrealism, where the ropes and the head bound together in an unusual manner intensify and renew an image of the hanged man. And what could furnish a better psychological portrait than the turkey that produces its own medals in *A Great Man for Small Affairs?* In every poster, man is transformed into something else, something that will better express his psychological essence.

Aiming at surrealism of a more complex nature, Górowski creates images that can be placed in a series through juxtaposition. In *A Glance into the Studio* a man is drawing a man who is drawing another man. Other examples are provided by *Our God's Brother* and by the two heroes of *The Story of the Soldier*.

Architecture, painting, sculpture, psychology and his long-standing activity as a collector of folk artifacts have all contributed to form Górowski's artistic personality. His academic experience, intensified by personal emotions, results in a powerful surrealist and expressionist visual style. As one of his country's most original and prolific creators, Górowski has contributed profoundly to the high quality of the Polish poster today.

230点余りのポスターに見られるグロフスキーの芸術は、独特な心理的世界の描写で世界中に知られるようになった。その心理的世界とはオークル、土の色の世界である。大地のような根源的なものを好む彼が、それを強調するためにこの色を使うのである。

彼のポスターに描かれた物は、身の回りにある、ベーシックでシンプルなものばかりである。彼はこれらの物の持つテクスチュアに執着する。彫刻や絵画を学んでいた頃は、紙や木、皮、布、それに金属まで使って制作を試みていた。例えば作品「警察」の原画は、同ポスターの半分ほどの大きさの錆びた鉄板に直接施されている。

グロフスキーは生来一つの物を画面一杯に大きく描くのが好きであるが、その傾向を彼独自の作風にまで高めたのは、クラクフ美術アカデミー建築学科在籍中のことである。当時のことを彼は次のように述べている。「ある日教授から、大きな平面に置かれたいくつかの木片を縮尺で製図するように言われたが、無意識に寸法をかなり大きくしてしまった」。「ジェレニア・グラでのスペイン文化との出会い」や「光の方へ」などの作品はその表われである。

オークルとその色調、物のテクスチュア、大きな形状に対する愛着は、彼のポスター制作の生の材料であると言えよう。グロフスキーは常に、人生の素晴らしさや日々の労苦、人間により引き起こされる不幸などを表現する新しい、独特な方法を求め続けている。

グロフスキーは、彼の求めるダイナミックな表現にぴったり合った感情的エネルギーを演劇に見出した。「アンティゴネー」に描かれた、身体を突き抜けて地面に縛り付けるロープは、悲劇的な運命の力の斬新な象徴である。このロープは身体を縛り付けるだけでなく、手足を突き抜け、その苦しさを分かちあえる人にまで届く。

グロフスキーの世界は人間が中心である。このアーティストは基本的コンセプトの源となる、一風変わった組み合わせを見出そうとする。「警察」の縛られた顔は、シュールレアリズムの素晴らしい例である。ロープと頭との関係が異常であり、絞首刑の男のイメージを強烈で新たなものにしている。勲章を自家増殖する七面鳥を描いた「くだらないことにおいて偉い男」ほど、心理描写の優れた作品はないのではないだろうか。グロフスキーのどのポスターでも、人間が、その心理をより鮮明に示す何か別のものに変身している。

グロフスキーは、より複雑なシュールレアリズムを目指して、何枚か並べて張ると面白い効果の出るようなイメージを創造している。「アトリエ瞥見」では、画家が1人の男を描いているが、2枚並べてみると、画中の男も別の男を描いているように見える。「我が主の兄弟」や、「兵士の物語」の2人のヒーローたちも、そうした例である。

建築、絵画、彫刻、心理学そして長年の民芸品蒐集といったすべてのことがらが、グロフスキーの芸術的パーソナリティ形成の一助となっている。彼の感情に裏打ちされた学問的経験は、シュールレアリストと表現主義者としての力強い視覚スタイルを作り出した。今日ポーランドのポスターは、その質を高く評価されているが、グロフスキーは最も独特かつ多作なポスター作家の一人として、これに大いなる貢献をしてきたのである。

1　"The Soldier's Story"「兵士の物語」1986

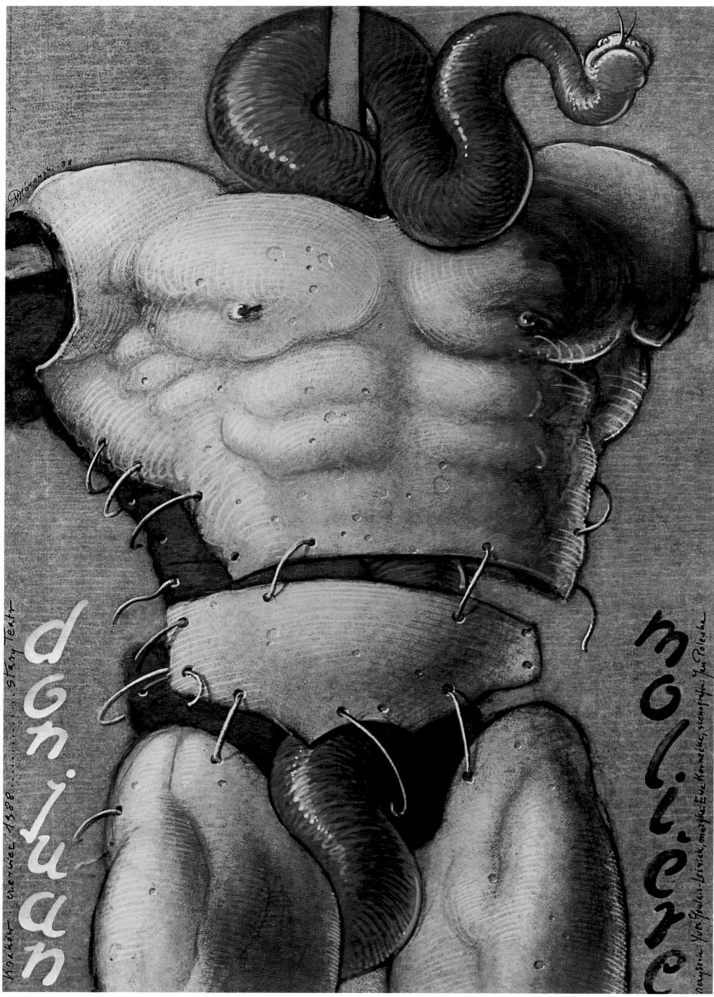

2 "Don Juan" 「ドン・ジュアン」 1988

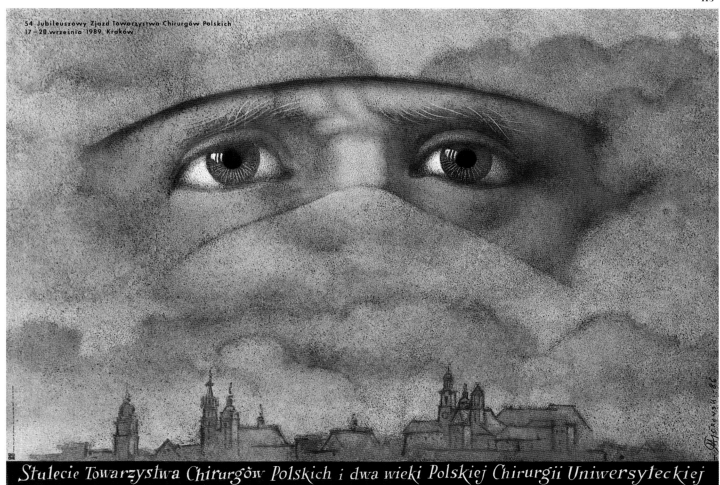

3 "Anniversaries of Polish University Surgery" 「ポーランドの大学外科記念祭」1986

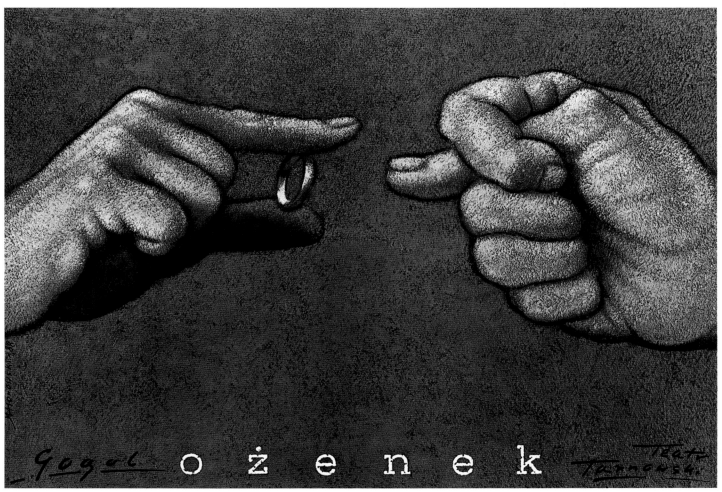

4 "The Marriage" 「結婚」1988

5 "Growski Poster Exhibition" 「グロフスキーポスター展」 1988

6 "Toward the Light" 「光の方へ」 1989

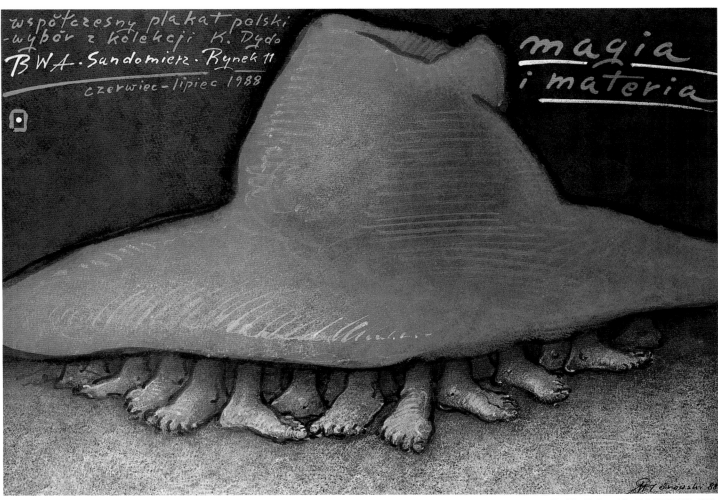

7 "The Magic and Reality" 「幻想と現実」 1988

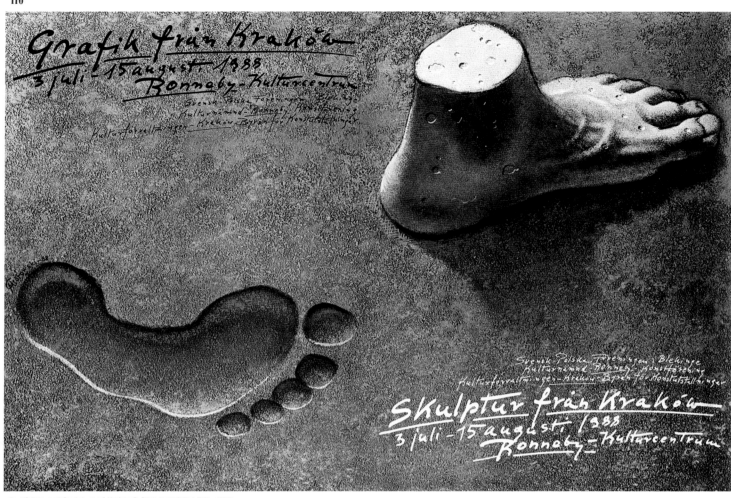

8 "Prints and Sculpture of Krakow" 「クラクフの版画と彫刻」 1988

9 "By Foot" 「歩いて」 1989

10 "The Miser"「守銭奴」1987

11 "Sculpture of the Year '88"「88年度最優秀彫刻」1989

12 "Old Times" 「昔」 1984

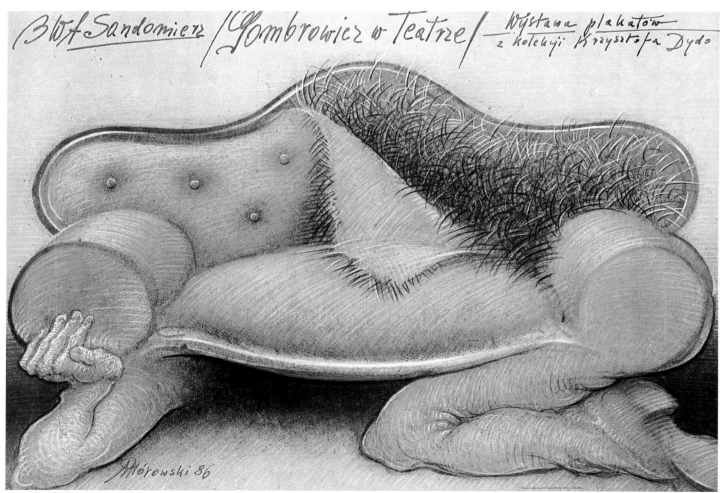

13 "Playwright Gombrowicz" 「劇作家ゴンブロウィッツ」 1986

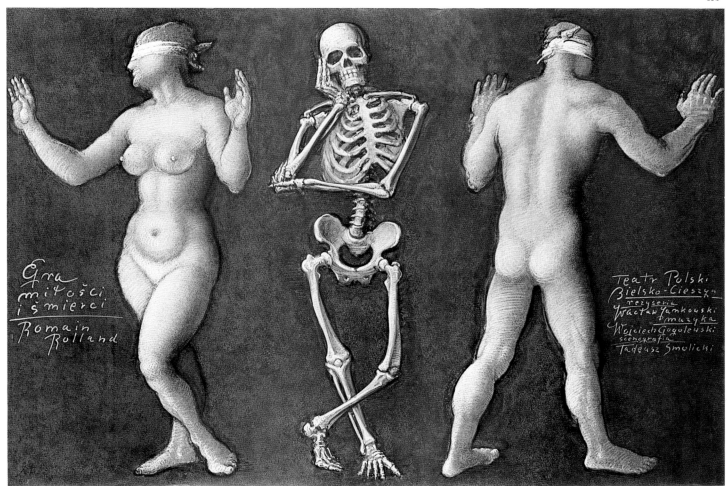

14 "A Game of Love and Death" 「愛と死の戯れ」 1988

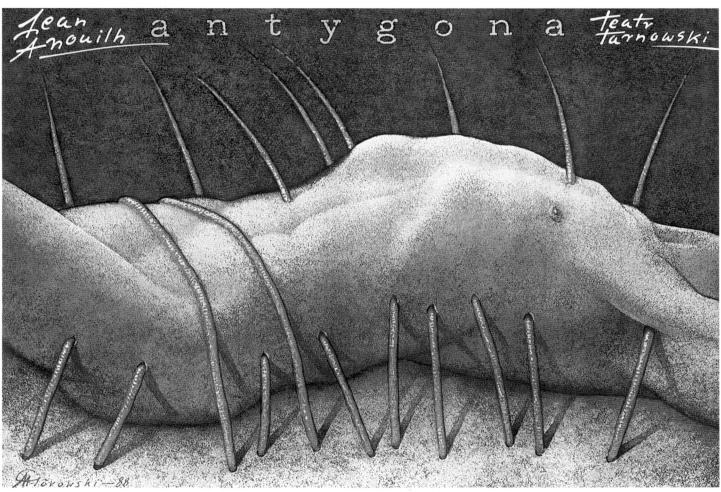

15 "Antigone" 「アンティゴネー」 1988

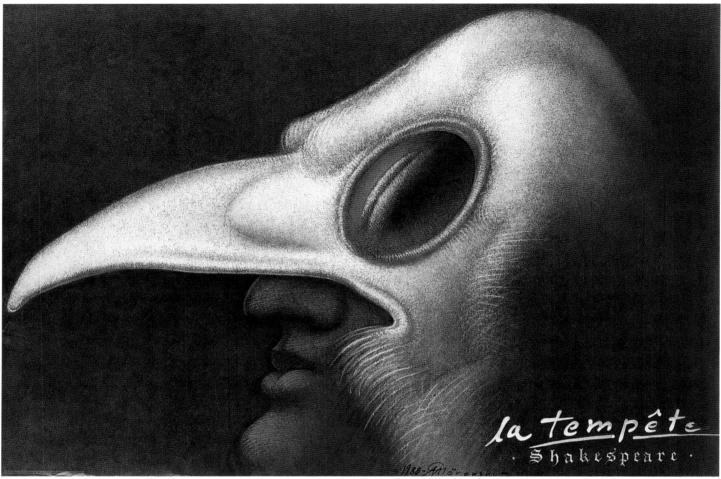

16 "The Tempest" 「嵐」 1988

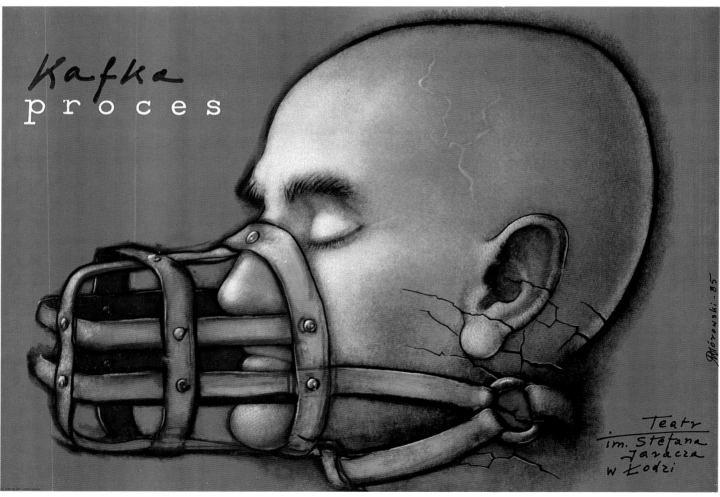

17 "The Trial" 「審判」 1985

– Adam Raczkowski – Kraków, ul. Stolarska 17 –

Galeria
młyn

18　"Mill Gallery"「ミル・ギャラリー」1985

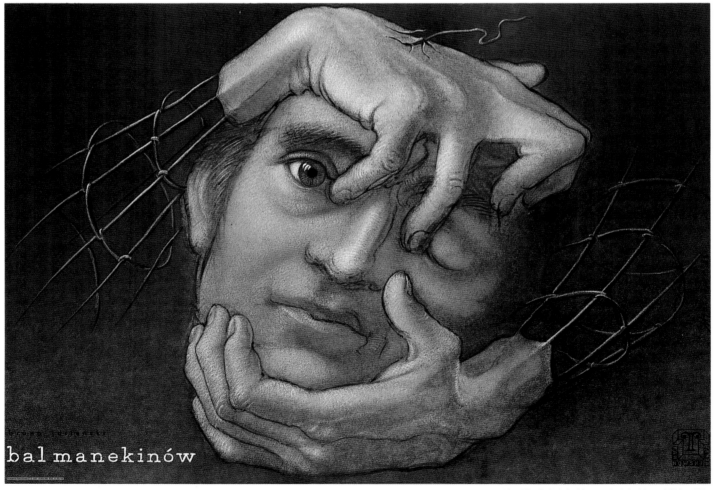

bal manekinów

19　"The Ball of the Mannequins"「マネキンの舞踏会」1986

21 "Stanislaw and Bogumil" 「スタニスラフとボグミル」 1978

TEATR
IM. J. SŁOWACKIEGO
W KRAKOWIE
KAROL
WOJTYŁA
REŻYSERIA
KRYSTYNA SKUSZANKA
SCENOGRAFIA
ANNA SEKUŁA
GRAŻYNA ŻUBROWSKA
MUZYKA
KRZYSZTOF PENDERECKI
BRAT NASZEGO BOGA

TEATR
IM. J. SŁOWACKIEGO
W KRAKOWIE
KAROL
WOJTYŁA
REŻYSERIA
KRYSTYNA SKUSZANKA
SCENOGRAFIA
ANNA SEKUŁA
GRAŻYNA ŻUBROWSKA
MUZYKA
KRZYSZTOF PENDERECKI
BRAT NASZEGO BOGA

22-23　"The Brother of Our God"「我らが主の兄弟」1980　　　　　23

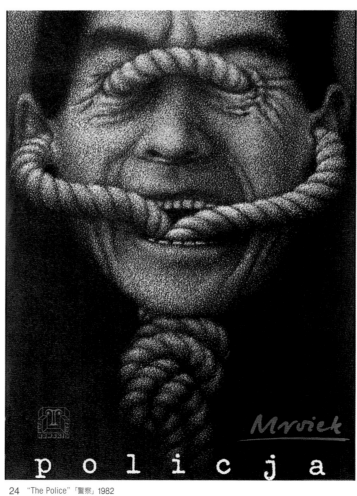

24　"The Police"「警察」1982

PIERWSZY DZIEŃ LEON WOLNOSCI KRUCZKOWSKI

REŻYSERIA: EWA KUTRYŚ·SCENOGRAFIA: ANNA SEKUŁA

TEATR IM. JULIUSZA SŁOWACKIEGO W KRAKOWIE

25 "The First Day of Freedom" 「自由最初の日」1979

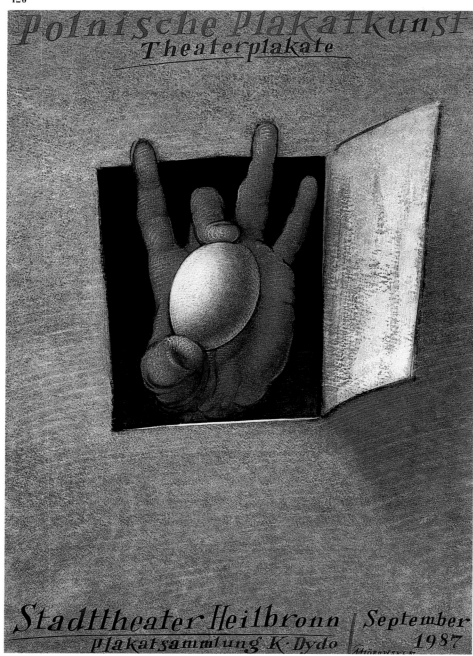

26 "Poster Art in Poland" 「ポーランドのポスターアート」1987

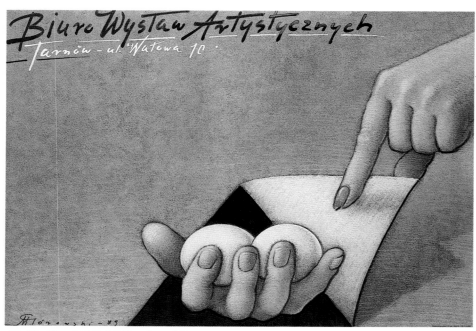

27 "The Office of Artistic Exhibition—Tarnow" 「タルヌフ芸術展局」1989

28 "Allan Rzepka—Painting"「アラン・ルゼプカの絵画」1988

29 "The World's Best Posters" 「世界のベストポスター」 1988

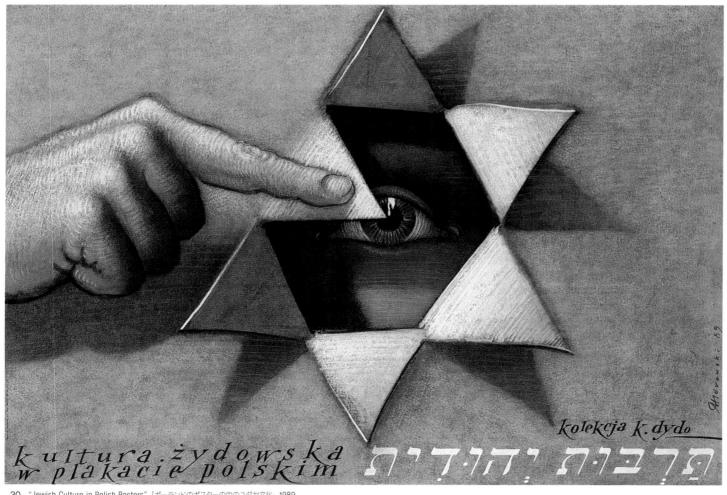

30 "Jewish Culture in Polish Posters" 「ポーランドのポスターの中のユダヤ文化」 1989

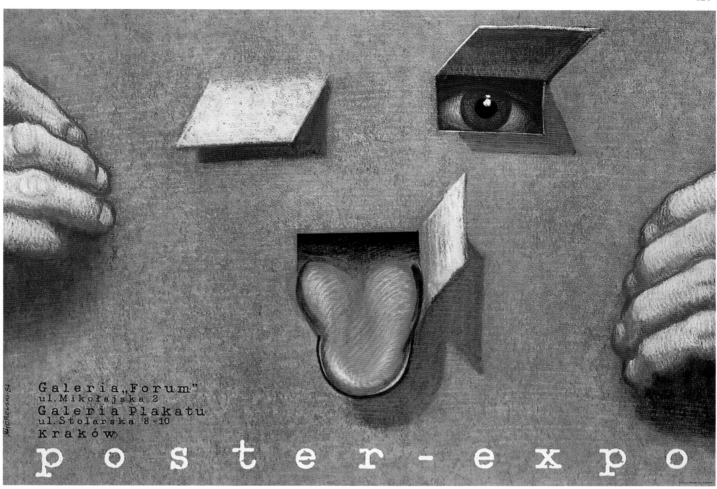

31 "Poster Expo"「ポスター・エキスポ」1984

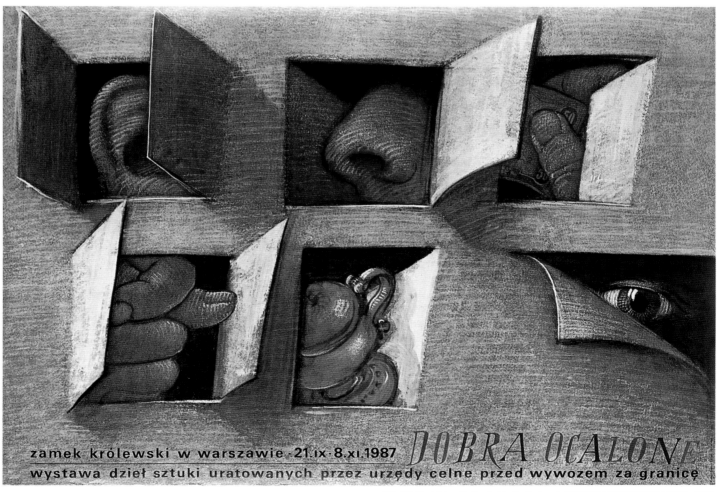

32 "Heritage Items Confiscated by the Customs"「税関に没収され国外散逸を免れた文化財」1987

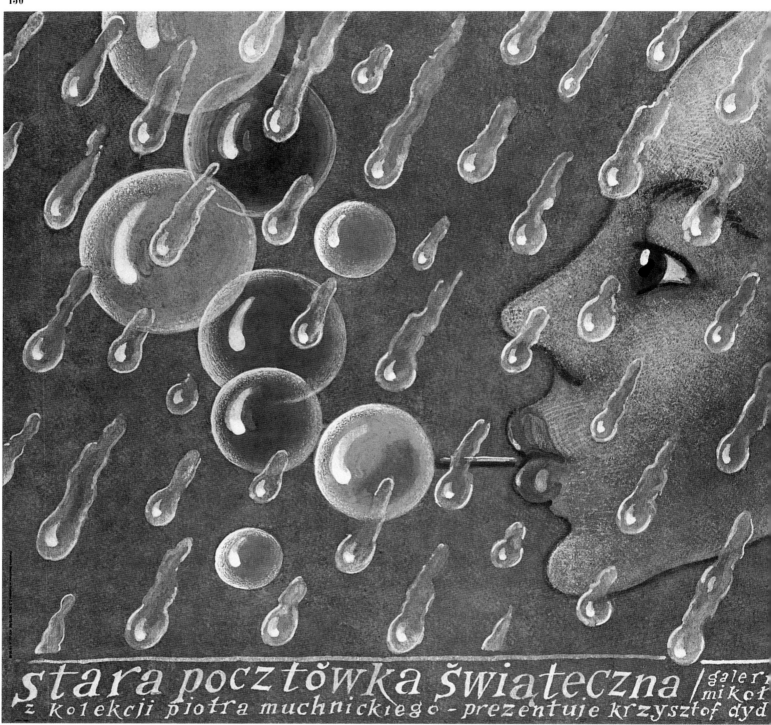

33 "Old Postcard for a Holiday" 「古い祭日用の葉書」 1986

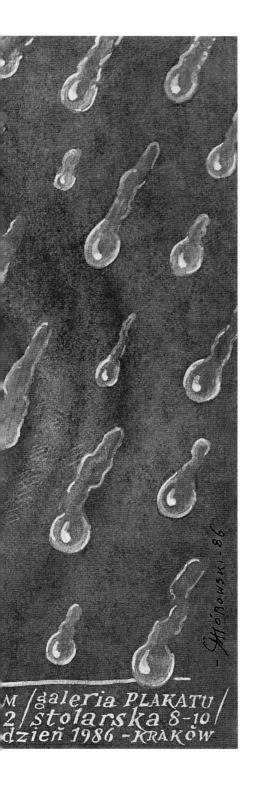

34 "Jewish Society" 「ユダヤ人社会」 1988

35 "French Culture in Polish Posters" 「ポーランドポスターの中のフランス文化」 1985

36 "T. Lautrec—The Great Poster Creator" 「T. ロートレック─偉大なポスター作家」 1988

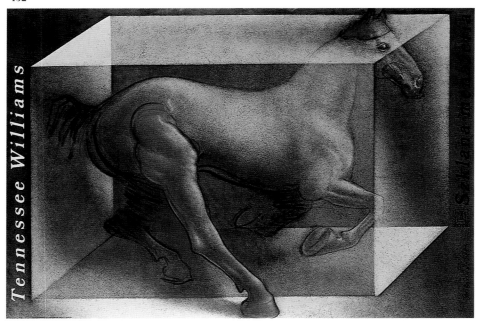

37 "Glass Menagerie"「ガラスの動物園」1985

38 "Tarnow Theater"「タルヌフ劇場」1988

39 "You May Have It"「この船あげます」1988

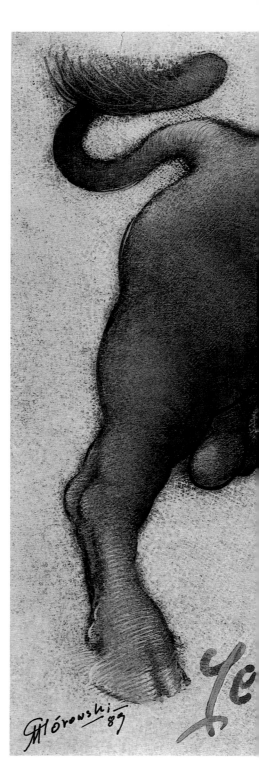

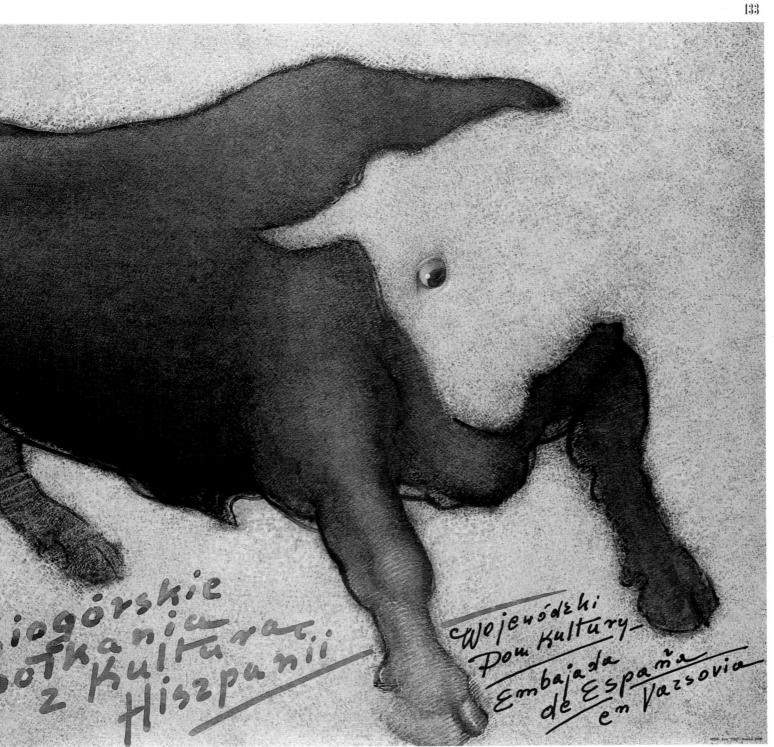

40　"Encounter with Spanish Culture in Jelenia Gora"「ジェレニア・グラでのスペイン文化との出会い」1989

FRED OTNES フレッド・オトネス

Mitsuo Katsui 勝井三雄

Fred Otnes originally pursued a career as a "conventional" illustrator. Then in 1960 his career, and his life, took a decisive turn after a friend chanced to lend him a book of etchings to browse. From that moment on he began to find fascination working with collages. Though I had previously seen three or four of his collage works in magazines or wherever, this is the first time I have seen over 40 items together at once—and as a congregated whole they strike me all the more alluring.

If I had to select my very favorite of Otnes's works, it would be the illustration he did for a Franklin Library book in 1984. The work shows a human collage of large and small photos and negatives, with a dividing line passing vertically down the center to generate a sense of acute tension. The resulting face, eerily sliced into two halves, reminds me of an expressionless Noh mask.

Nearly all of Otnes's works contain human figures, either face forward or in profile. And in virtually each of them portions are concealed, either covered by something else or purposefully cut away. From these unseen areas emerge psychological spaces that invite hypothesis or speculation, and in this way they create a crowning aura of intelligent pleasure.

The success of Otnes's collages lies in their integration of the unexpected, in the brilliant skill with which they juxtapose intrinsically alien objects. The past and the future. The macroscopic and the microscopic. Photographic positives and negatives. The two-dimensional and the three. The organic and the inorganic. The abstract and the concrete. The eternal and the momentary. By intertwining specific examples of these polar opposites, Otnes succeeds in creating a world altogether his own.

His procedure is quite time-consuming. He begins by pasting bits of pictures, paper scraps and cuttings from printed works directly on his canvas. The result he then sprays with dashes of color using an air-brush. Finally, he transforms his work to a print, even relying on embossing in order to recreate the uneven surfaces of the original.

I am particularly attracted to Otnes's works owing to a personal fondness I have long had for small woodblocks used to print encyclopedias and such in Europe during the 18th and 19th centuries. For a time I collected as many of these works as I could, from scientific tomes on animals and plants to compendiums of arithmetic symbols. I often relied on these works as materials for my designs.

Otnes's works are in many ways quite like them. They are collections of treasures from the past: patterns from paper currency, symbols used to analyze mathematic principles, bits of timeless paintings, computer graphics from TV screens. With musical resonance they carry messages from days of yore to the present, and blend into a nostalgic sepia tint with powerfully emotive force. They open up an infinite chain of doors inside our minds, allowing us to peer inside them in a frenzied attempt to unlock their secrets. There we discover the memories of our dreams, like afterimages of still photographs. Layer upon layer, the collages of Fred Otnes resurrect the fragments of awareness that lie buried in our minds.

夢の中の記憶は、1枚の印象的なスチール写真のような残像である。フレッド・オトネスの扱う材料は、われわれの脳裏に記憶された断片を1枚1枚取り出して重層するコラージュである。

典型的なイラストレーターとして制作に没頭していた彼に、ある日友人が1冊のエッチングの本を貸してくれた。その本は、その後の彼の人生を決定的なものにしたらしい。1960年のことであった。今回、40点余りの作品を一度に見た。以前雑誌の記事などで見て3、4点は記憶に残っていたが、その表現の緻密な構成とエッチング風の作風には一層強く魅せられてしまった。

彼の作品の中で、私が好きなものを1点選ぶとすれば、なんといってもフランクリン・ライブラリーのための本のイラスト(1984)であろう。それは大小のネガとポジの人物像の組み合わせで、中央を切る1本の線が画面の緊張感を引き出し、この正面を2つに切られ結合された顔からは、堅く無表情な能面を連想させられる。彼のほとんどの作品の中に人物像が組み入れられているが、そのいずれもが正面あるいは横を向き、必ずといってよいほど、その一部がなにかで覆われ、または切り取られ隠されている。そこには自ずと推定や憶測といった心理空間が生まれ、知的な快感を演出するもととなっている。

彼のコラージュの秘密は異質なものの組み合わせによる意外性であり、そうした対比を駆使した見事さにある。過去と未来、巨視と微視、ネガティブとポジティブ、立体と平面、生態と無機、抽象と具象、悠久と刹那といった、いくつもの事がらを複雑に組み合わせることにより彼独自の世界を演出しているのである。

混沌としたその画面は、写真であったり、スクラップや印刷物の切り抜きであったり、これを直接張り込むことはもちろん、エアブラシで補色し、更に印刷で刷り込むといった手の込んだ技法から、凹凸をつけるエンボスの技法まで使用するやり方で表現されている。

以前私は、18〜19世紀に出版された百科事典等の小口木版に秘められたヨーロッパの理性と感性にひかれていた。これらの科学的観察図鑑類の動植物から数学記号に至るものまで収集し、デザイン材料として好んでつかっていたこともあって、オトネスの作品には目をとめていた。

彼の作品に接すると、あたかも博物誌の世界に入り込んでしまったかのように、未知の扉を1枚1枚開いて脳裏を覗き込み、謎を解き明かしたいという衝動に取りつかれる。彼の作品は紙幣の紋様、数理を解析する記号、長い時間を閉じ込めた絵画の一部、ブラウン管に現われたCGパターン等、どんな微細な部分でも精緻な表現でかたち造られた過去の大いなる遺産の集積であり、中世から現代へのメッセージが精妙な音楽的共振を伴って伝わってくる。張り詰めた画面は見事な垂直的構成の中で結晶化し、セピア調の色彩で調和している。そこからは、作者の意図が離れがたい感動となって伝わってくる。

私は久し振りに心を高揚させられた。それは、私自身の宝箱を開けるような、心のときめきを奮いおこされたからかもしれない。

1 Book illustration 本のイラストレーション 1984

2 Book illustration 本のイラストレーション 1983

3 Promotion piece PR作品 1986

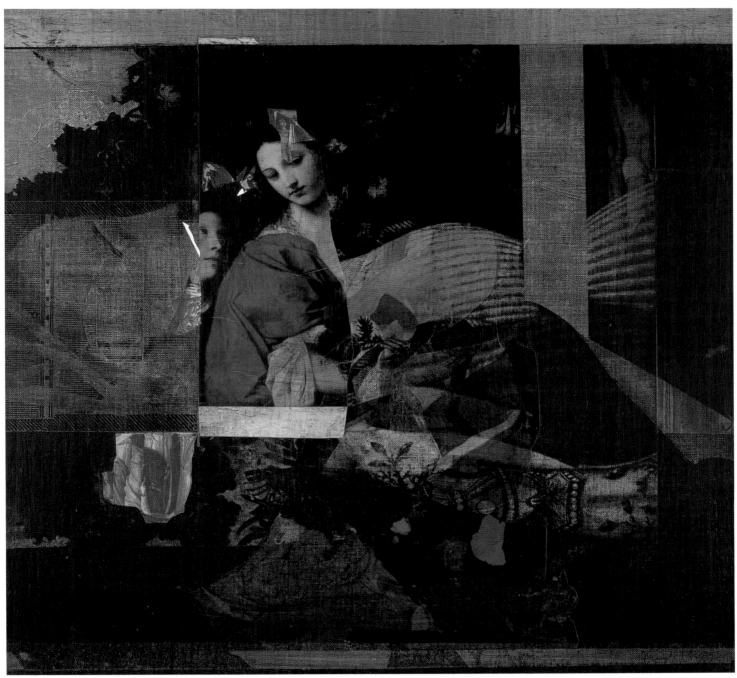

4　Magazine illustration　雑誌のイラストレーション　1988

5   Self promotion advertising 自己PR広告 1988

6 Poster for one-man show 個展ポスター 1982

7 Magazine cover 雑誌の表紙 1989

8 Illustrators workshop advertising piece イラストレーターズワークショップの広告 1980

9 Portrait for magazine 雑誌のためのポートレート 1980

10 Editorial illustration イラストレーション 1986

12 Unpublished magazine cover 雑誌の表紙(未発表) 1988

13 Magazine illustration 雑誌のイラストレーション 1983

14 Annual report 年鑑 1979

15 Magazine cover 雑誌の表紙 1987

16 Brochure for company 企業パンフレット 1986

17　Annual report 年鑑 1987

18 Experimental collage コラージュ試作 1989

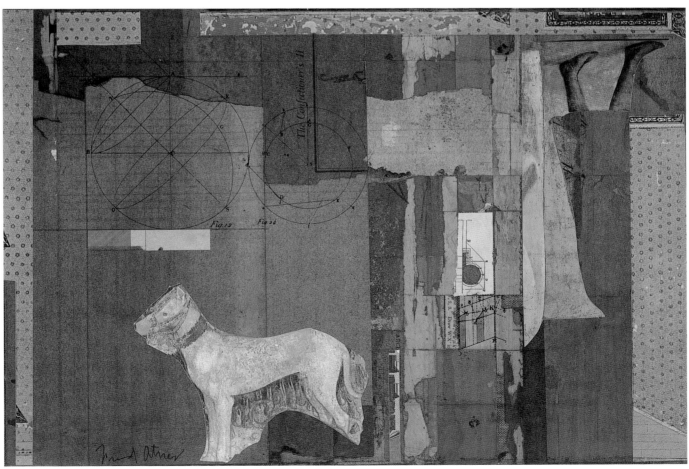

19 Self promotion piece 自己PR作品 1989

22 Brochure related to American Bicentennial アメリカ建国200年記念パンフレット 1977

23 Advertising for high-tech company ハイテク企業の広告 1989

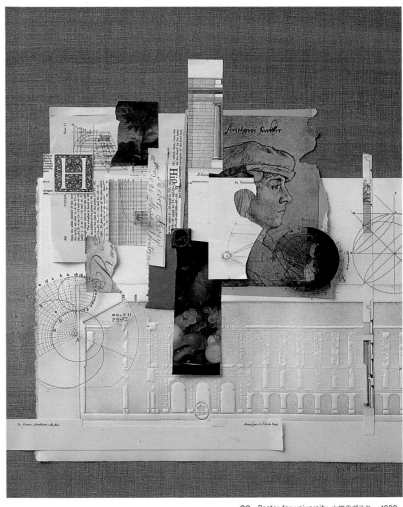

26 Poster for university 大学のポスター 1989

27 Advertising piece 広告 1988

28 Book cover 本の表紙 1987

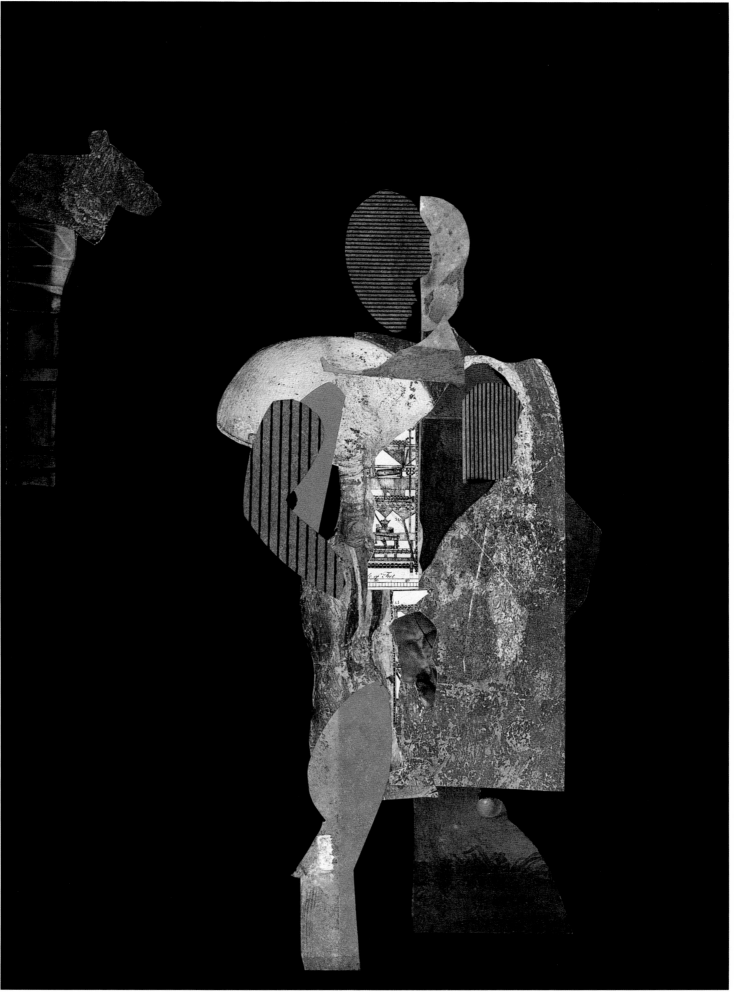

29 Collage figure コラージュ 1989

Editor's Viewpoint 編集者の視点

PICASSO'S **PIERRETTE'S WEDDING** ピカソ ピエレットの婚礼

Yusaku Kamekura 亀倉雄策

The year was 1905. Picasso was but a youth of 24, caught in a brief transition between his "blue period" and his "rose." Incomplete records suggested that he had produced a grand masterpiece to bridge the two periods, and a small black-and-white illustration had even been found. Nevertheless the work itself had vanished, and consensus was that the painting must have been lost in a fire.

But there it was! Stockholm, 1988, part of a showing of Picasso's works. And grand indeed it was: 115×195cm in size. Picasso admirers were excited not just by the discovery itself, but by the fact that the newfound work depicted a familiar theme of Picasso's blue period: itinerant entertainers on life's back streets. Entitled *Les Noces de Pierrette* (Pierrette's Wedding), the painting poignantly describes a clown, deeply enamored of Pierrette, throwing his love a farewell kiss as she becomes the unwilling bride of a wealthy old man. The work no doubt elicits different associations in each who views it. In my case this long, horizontal painting reminds me, perhaps imprudently, of da Vinci's *The Last Supper*.

The work is drawn in oil paints which have been dilluted in turpentine. The result gives off the airy lightness of watercolors, with large portions of the canvas showing through. Still, the critical areas of the work are done in realistic detail, far beyond the common skill of a 24-year-old. To be sure, despite his youth Picasso was already a grand master of his art.

Rumor has it that the work had lain hidden in a bank vault in Paris for over half a century, deposited there by a Swedish collector. Upon his death, the heirs decided to auction it off in order to pay inheritance taxes. For a period of three days only, the painting was brought to Tokyo and put on display for a limited viewing, as a preview to the auction. As soon as I saw the work, I immediately asked Mr. Yamamoto, president of the Fuji TV Gallery where the showing took place, for permission to photograph it. With his gracious approval, I was able to produce the photographic reproductions that appear in these pages, including close-up shots.

The auction itself took place via simultaneous satellite broadcast between Paris and Tokyo on November 30, 1989. Paris time was 10 am; Tokyo time, 6 pm. The broadcast from Paris showed a packed audience projected on a large screen. The Tokyo venue was also filled to capacity, brimming with eager anticipation. Bidding started at nearly $17 million. Quickly it jumped to over $35 million, then $44 million, and right on up to $47 million. Finally, a bid was heard for more than $51 million, the highest sum ever offered for a work of art.

The Paris and Tokyo auction rooms were hushed in tense anticipation. Then the auctioneer raised his mallet and declared that if no higher bid was heard in Paris, the sale would go to Tokyo. A rustle stirred through the Paris audience, but no voice was raised. The mallet came down. Applause broke out. The sale of the century had taken no more than 4 minutes to conclude. To me it seemed like more than half an hour.

これは、衝撃的な事件だった。

1905年というとピカソが24歳。青の時代から赤の時代に移行する僅かな間だった。この間隙を埋めるような大作をピカソが描いていたという断片的な記録が、白黒の小さな図版と共に確認されていた。しかし、それ以降の行方は幻となり、火災で焼失したという風説さえたっていた。それが、1988年のストックホルムのピカソ展に、忽然と出現したのである。しかも115×195cmという大作である。さらにピカソ・ファンを狂喜させたのは、青の時代のテーマ、人生の裏通りを行く旅芸人の結婚式が描かれていたことであった。「ピエレットの婚礼」というタイトルのこの絵には、金持ちの老人に結婚を強いられたピエレットに、彼女に想いを寄せるピエロがお別れの悲しい投げキッスをするというドラマが哀愁を込めて描かれている。しかしこの絵は、見る人によって、それぞれ別のストーリーを思い浮ばせるに違いない。私は私で、この横長の構図を持った祝宴から、ダビンチの「最後の晩餐」を不謹慎にも連想してしまった。

ピカソは、油絵具をテレピン油で薄めて水彩画のようにさらりと仕上げている。だからカンバス地が透けて見える部分が多い。でも急所はしっかりと写実の技法で締めている点、とても24歳の制作とは思われず、すでに巨匠の風格を持っているのに驚かされる。

この絵は、一説によるとスウェーデンのコレクターがパリの銀行の金庫に、半世紀以上も秘蔵していたという。そのコレクターの死によって、遺族が相続税のためにオークションにかける決心をしたということである。その「ピエレットの婚礼」が、東京で限られた人々のために3日間だけ展示され、すぐパリに持ち帰られてしまった。私は、この絵の前に立って、すぐに、この絵を展示したフジテレビギャラリーの山本社長に、この絵の撮影を依頼した。画面全体と部分トリミングの撮影である。今、この誌上でお目に掛けているのは、山本社長のご好意によるものだ。

1989年11月30日に、衛星テレビ中継によって、パリと東京で同時にオークションが開催された。3日間の東京展示は、このためのプレビューだったのだ。オークションはパリが午前10時、東京は午後6時の時差で同時に開始された。会場の大画面の映像には、パリの会場の生々しい超満員の情景がとらえられていた。東京の会場も超満員で熱気がひしひしと迫って感じられた。いよいよ待ちに待った「ピエレットの婚礼」のオークションが開始された。競りのスタートは23億6千万円。やがてパリが50億円の値をつけた。すぐに62億円にはね上った。またたく間にパリが66億円の値をつけた。会場は、溜め息で大きくゆれた。そして、遂に71億7千万円という史上最高の値がつけられた。パリも東京も、シーンと水を打ったような緊張感が張りつめた。

競り師が、木槌をふり上げ「パリから、これ以上の声がかからなければ、東京に槌をうちますよ」と呼びかけた。パリからはどよめきだけで、遂に声はあがらなかった。バシッと木槌が机を叩いた。会場から、わっとばかりの拍手。この世紀の槌の音がするまで、わずか4分間の勝負だった。しかし、私には30分以上もかかったように思われた。

"Pierrette's Wedding"「ピエレットの婚礼」1905

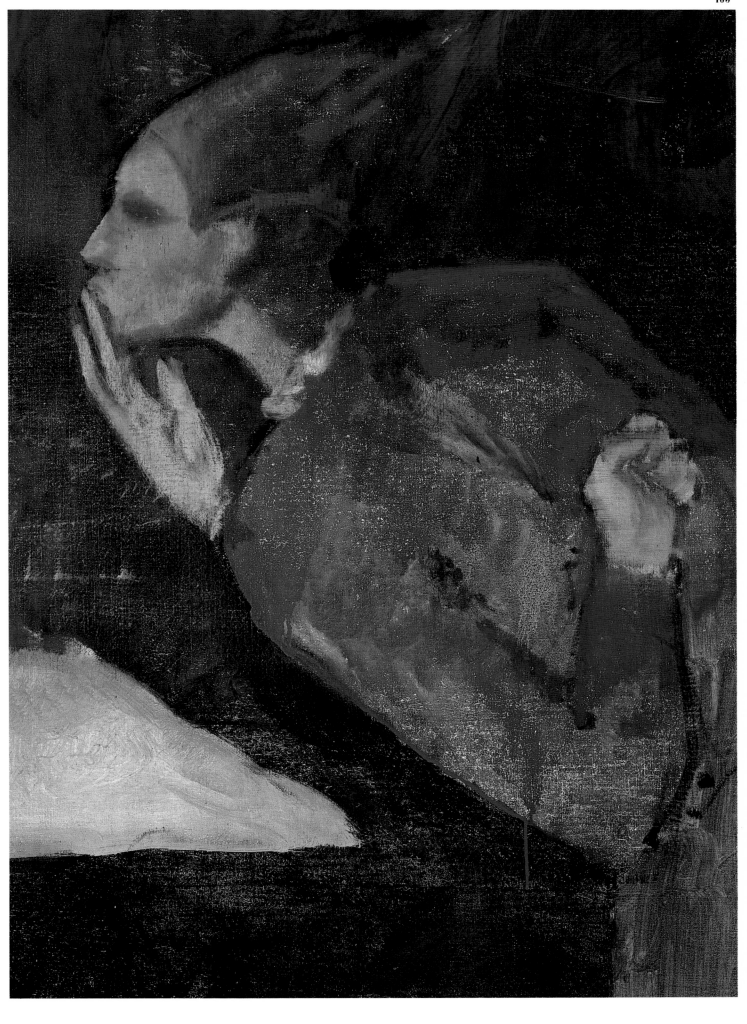

ARTISTS' PROFILES
作家略歴

JEAN-MICHEL FOLON
ジャン゠ミッシェル・フォロン

FRANCE
1934- Born in Brussels, Belgium. 1955- Discontinues his architectural education and moves near Paris to pursue design studies. 1960- His works are accepted by *Esquire* and *The New Yorker* magazines. 1965- Receives Grand Prize at the 3rd Humor in Art Triennale in Italy. 1966- Receives Certificate of Merit from the New York Art Directors Club. 1967- His works appear in *Time, Fortune* and *Graphis*. 1968- Creates a 36m² panel, featuring 500 lights, for the Milan Triennale. Prepares a book for the New York Museum of Modern Art. 1969- Holds first showing in New York, at the Lefebre Gallery. 1970- Visits Japan and holds one-man show in Tokyo. Participates in 35th Venice Biennale, at Belgium pavilion. 1971- Exhibition at the Museum of Decorative Arts in Paris. 1972- One-man shows at the Arts Club of Chicago and the Grand-Palais in Paris. 1973- Prepares illustrations for Kafka's *Metamorphosis*, published by Olivetti. Publishes a collection of original lithographs, with a preface written by Max Ernst. Receives Grand Prize at the 12th São Paulo Biennale. 1974- His works become the subject of an essay published by Giorgio Soavi. 1975- Prepares a mural for Waterloo Station in London, for Olivetti. 1976- One-man shows in Rotterdam and Essen. 1978- Publishes a book on his works, with an introduction written by Milton Glaser. 1979- Provides illustrations for a book by Ray Bradbury. 1981- Creates video images for Stravinsky's *The Story of the Soldier*. 1983- Produces animated films, which are shown widely in the United States. 1984- Furnishes illustrations for a book of poems by Guillaume Apollinaire. Exhibits watercolors at the Picasso Museum in Antibes. 1985- Visits Japan for a retrospective showing of his works, which subsequently tours nationwide for 18 months. Exhibits 200 works in Venice. 1987- Creates poster for reopening of Teatro Olimpico. Holds 2-man show, together with Milton Glaser, at the Museum of Fine Arts in Buenos Aires. 1988- Creates symbol mark for bicentennial of the French Revolution. Provides illustration for declaration of human rights, for Amnesty International. 1989- Designs stage settings for a comedy by Goldini, in Venice and Rome. Prepares posters for "Flying Spirit" exhibition held in conjunction with French bicentennial celebration. Provides illustrations for human rights declaration.

フランス
1934ーブリュッセル生まれ。1955ー建築の勉強を止めてパリ近郊に移り、デザインに打ち込む。1960ーアメリカの雑誌「エスクァイア」、「ニューヨーカー」などに作品が採用される。1965ーイタリア第3回ユーモア芸術トリエンナーレで大賞受賞。1966ーニューヨークADC奨励賞受賞。1967ー「タイム」、「フォーチュン」が作品を採用、「グラフィス」で紹介される。1968ーミラノトリエンナーレのために500個のライトのついた36㎡のパネルを制作。ニューヨーク近代美術館の依頼で本を作成。1969ーニューヨーク、ルフェーブルギャラリーで個展。1970ー訪日、東京で個展。第35回ベネチアビエンナーレベルギー館に出品。1971ーパリ装飾美術館で個展。1972ーシカゴアートクラブとパリグランパレで個展。1973ーオリベッティ発行のカフカ「変身」のイラストレーションを描く。オリジナルリトグラフ集

を出版、マックス・エルンストに序文を書いてもらう。第12回サンパウロビエンナーレに出品、大賞受賞。1974ージョルジュ・ソアビがフォロンの作品についてのエッセイ集「遮られる心配のない展望」を出版。1975ーオリベッティの依頼でロンドンのウォーテルロー駅の壁画を制作。1976ーロッテルダム、エッセンで個展。1978ー「フォロンのポスター」を出版、ミルトン・グレーザーが序文を書く。1979ーブラッドベリーの「火星の回想記」の挿絵。1981ーストラヴィンスキーの「兵士の物語」を映像化する。1983ーアニメ映画を制作、アメリカ各地で上映される。1984ーアポリネールの詩に挿絵をつける。ピカソ美術館で水彩画展。1985ー日本で回顧展、各地を18か月間巡回。ベニスの美術館で回顧展。1987ーオリンピコ劇場再開のためのポスター制作。ブエノスアイレスのグラセ美術館でミルトン・グレイザーと2人展を開催。1988ーフランス革命200年祭のシンボルマークを制作。アムネスティの依頼で人権宣言のイラストレーションを描く。1989ーベニスとローマでゴルディニのコメディの舞台装置を制作。フランス革命200年祭の「飛翔する精神展」ポスター制作。「世界人権宣言」のイラストレーションを手掛ける。

KATSURA FUNAKOSHI
舟越 桂

JAPAN
1951   Born in Morioka.
1975   Graduated from Tokyo University of Art and Design.
1977   Graduated from Postgraduate Course of Tokyo National University of Fine Arts and Music.
1982   One-man show at Gallery Okabe, Tokyo.
1985   One-man show at Nishimura Gallery, Tokyo.
1985-87   Lecturer at Tokyo National University of Fine Arts and Music.
1986-87   Resided in London on special grant awarded by Japanese Agency for Cultural Affairs.
1988   One-man show at Nishimura Gallery, Tokyo.

1951   盛岡に生まれる
1975   東京造形大学彫刻学科卒業
1977   東京芸術大学大学院美術研究科彫刻専修了
1982   ギャラリー・オカベ(東京)にて個展
1985   西村画廊(東京)にて個展
1985-87   東京芸術大学彫刻科非常勤講師
1986-87   文化庁芸術家在外研修員として1年ロンドンに滞在
1988   西村画廊(東京)にて個展

OTL AICHER
オトル・アイヒャー

WEST GERMANY
1922 Born in Ulm.
1946 Studied sculpture at the Academy of Munich.
1949 Initiator and founding committee member of the Design School of Ulm.
1954 Lecturer in the Department of Visual Communication.
Honorable Prize at the Milan Triennale.
1955 Prize for best German posters.
1958 First Prize for typography in Innsbruck.
1962-64 Rector of the school.
1967-72 Graphic designer for the Olympic Games in Munich, development of a worldwide system of pictograms.
——— Development of corporate identity for Braun Electrical Appliances, Deutsche Lufthansa, ZDF Television, Frankfurt Airport, etc.

西ドイツ
1922 ウルム生まれ
1946 ミュンヘンアカデミーで彫刻を学ぶ
1949 ウルム造形大学設立メンバー
1954 視覚伝達学科の講師をつとめる
ミラノトリエンナーレ佳作
1955 ドイツベストポスター賞
1958 インスブルックタイポグラフィー賞第1位
1962-64 ウルム造形大学学長をつとめる
1967-72 ミュンヘンオリンピックのグラフィックデザイナーとしてピクトグラムシステムを作成
その他主な仕事には、ブラウン、ルフトハンザ、ZDFテレビ、フランクフルト空港のCIデザインなどがある

NORIKO UENO
上野紀子

JAPAN
1940 Born in Saitama Pref.
1962 Graduated from Department of Fine Arts of Nippon University.
1967 Held one-man show in Ginza.

1972 Awarded Foreign Minister's Prize for *Microcosm* at Tokyo International Biennale.
1973 Held one-man show in Ginza.
Published *Elephant Buttons* from Harper & Row of New York.
1974-75 Did Illustration work for the *New York Times* and *New Yorker Magazine*.
1975 Received Culture Prize from Kodansha Publishing Co.
1982 Recommended three times for Culture Prize of Sankei Children's Publications.
1987 Received Japan Children's Book Prize.
1990 Currently working in children's book production; also delving into oil-painting.

1940 埼玉県生まれ
1962 日本大学芸術学部卒業
1967 銀座で個展
1972 「MICROCOSM」で東京国際ビエンナーレ外務大臣賞
1973 銀座で個展
ニューヨークでハーパー＆ロウ出版社から『ELEPHANT BUTTONS』出版
1974-75 ニューヨークで「ニューヨークタイムス」、「ニューヨークマガジン」のイラストの仕事を手がける
1975 講談社出版文化賞
1982 サンケイ児童出版文化賞推薦3回
1987 絵本にっぽん賞
—— 現在絵本の仕事を中心に油絵を描いている

ニューヨークでハーパー＆ロウ出版社から『ELEPHANT BUTTONS』出版

MIECZYSŁAW GÓROWSKI
ミェチスワフ・グロフスキー

POLAND
1941 Born in Nowy Sacz.
1955-59 Studied at State College of Fine Arts, Tarnów.
1959-66 Studied interior architecture, painting and industrial design at Academy of Fine Arts, Kraków.
1969 Grand Prize for Posters, Kraków.
1974-75 Grand Prizes at folkloric poster competitions, Kraków.
1976 Award of the Public, Kraków.
1976-77 Best Poster of the Year, Kraków.
1978 First Prize at exhibition of French Government Scholarship holders.
1979 Best Poster of the Year, Kraków.
1981 Awards at the 9th Polish Poster Biennale, Katowice.
1983 First Prize at the Colorado International Poster Exhibition.
"Individuality of the Year" Award from the Poster Collectors' Club, Poznań.
1985 Bronze Medal at the 1st International Poster Triennale, Toyama.
1986 Award at the 1st International Salon of Posters, Paris.
1987 Award at the 2nd International Salon of Posters, Paris.

Honorary award at the 1st ADC International Exhibition, New York.
Award at the 11th Polish Poster Biennale, Katowice.
1988 Head of Province Prize at the Theatres Festival, Tarnów.
Second Prize at the 16th Polish Review of Museum Posters, Przemyśl.
1989 Award from the Poster Collectors' Club, Poznań.
Awards at the 12th Polish Poster Biennale, Katowice.
Honorary award at the 18th International Poster Biennale, Lahti.

ポーランド
1941 ポーランドのノビソンチ生まれ
1955-59 タルヌフ美術大学で学ぶ
1959-66 クラクフ美術アカデミーで、内装建築、絵画、工業デザインを学ぶ
1969 クラクフポスター展グランプリ
1974・75 クラクフ民俗イベントポスター展グランプリ
1976 クラクフ市民賞
1976・77 クラクフベストポスターオブザイヤー
1978 フランス政府奨学生芸術展第1位
1979 クラクフベストポスターオブザイヤー
1981 第9回カトウィーツェポーランドポスタービエンナーレ入賞
1983 コロラド国際ポスタービエンナーレ第1位
ポズナニポスターコレクターズクラブ個人最高賞
1985 第1回世界ポスタートリエンナーレトヤマ銅賞
1986 第1回パリ国際ポスターサロン入賞
1987 第2回パリ国際ポスターサロン入賞
第1回ニューヨークADC国際展佳作
第12回カトウィーツェポーランドポスタービエンナーレ入賞
1988 タルヌフ演劇フェスティバルにおいて州知事賞
第16回プシェミシルポーランド美術館ポスター回顧展第2位
1989 ポズナニポスターコレクターズクラブ賞
第13回カトウィーツェポーランドポスタービエンナーレ入賞
第18回ラハティ国際ポスタービエンナーレ佳作

FRED OTNES
フレッド・オトネス

U.S.A.
Born in Kansas in 1926. After studying at the Chicago Art Institute and the American Academy, he began a career as an illustrator of magazines, books and advertising. His editorial clients have included *Life, Sports Illustrated, Atlantic Monthly, National Geographic, Fortune,* etc. Advertising clients include Exxon, GE, IBM, GM, 20th Century Fox, etc. He has won over 150 awards to date, including the "Hamilton King" and more than 50 other awards from the New York Society of Illustrators.

One-man shows
Museum of American Illustration (1973, 1976, 1982)
Arizona State University (1975)
GE Headquarters (1978)
Rhode Island School of Design (1982)
East Carolina University Museum of Art, Gray Art

Gallery (1982)
Spokane Community College (1982)
National Geographic Society (1988)

Collections
Boston Consulting Group, National Academy of
Sciences, IBM, New Britain Museum, Philip Morris,
20th Century Fox, National Parks Service, Aetna
Insurance, Reynolds Tobacco, American Express,
National Geographic Society, etc.

アメリカ
1926年カンザス生まれ。シカゴアートインスティチュートとアメリカ
ンアカデミーで学んだ後、雑誌、書籍、広告のイラストレーターとし
て活躍するようになる。出版関係の主なクライアントは、「ライフ」、
「スポーツイラストレーテッド」、「アトランティックマンスリー」、「ナシ
ョナルジオグラフィック」、「フォーチュン」など。広告関係では、エクソ
ン、GE、IBM、GM、20世紀フォックス社などがある。ハミルトンキン
グ賞をはじめとするニューヨークイラストレーター協会からの受賞が
50以上、その他100以上の受賞がある。

個展歴
アメリカイラストレーション美術館(1973、1976、1982年)
アリゾナ州立大学(1975年)
GE本社(1978年)
ロードアイランドスクールオブデザイン(1982年)
イーストカロライナ大学美術館グレイアートギャラリー(1982年)
スポケーンコミュニティカレッジ(1982年)
ナショナルジオグラフィックソサイエティ(1988年)

作品コレクション
ボストンコンサルティンググループ、米国科学アカデミー、IBM、新英
国美術館、フィリップモリス、20世紀フォックス、国立公園サービス、
エトナ保険、レイノルズたばこ、アメリカンエクスプレス、ナショナルジ
オグラフィックソサイエティなど

CONTRIBUTORS' PROFILES
評論執筆者紹介

GIORGIO SOAVI
Poet and novelist.

HIROSHI KOJITANI
Graphic designer. Vice-president of ICOGRADA.
Director of JAGDA.

TADAYASU SAKAI
Art critic. Vice-director of The Museum of Modern
Art, Kamakura.

SHUTARO MUKAI
Industrial designer. Professor of Musashino Art
University.

YOSHIAKI TONO
Art critic. Professor of Tama Art University.

RAYMOND VÉZINA
Art critic. Professor of Université du Québec à
Montréal.

MITSUO KATSUI
Graphic designer. Member of AGI and New York
ADC. Director of JAGDA.

YUSAKU KAMEKURA
Graphic designer. Member of AGI. President of
JAGDA and Japan Design Committee. Editor of
CREATION.

ジョルジオ・ソアビ
詩人、小説家

麹谷　宏
グラフィック・デザイナー
ICOGRADA副会長、JAGDA理事

酒井忠康
美術評論家
神奈川県立近代美術館副館長

向井周太郎
インダストリアルデザイナー
武蔵野美術大学教授

東野芳明
美術評論家
多摩美術大学教授

レイモン・ヴェジナ
デザイン史家
カナダケベック大学モントリオール校教授
グラフィックデザイン科ディレクター

勝井三雄
グラフィック・デザイナー
AGI会員、ニューヨークADC会員、JAGDA理事

亀倉雄策
グラフィック・デザイナー
AGI会員、JAGDA会長、日本デザインコミッティー 理事長
本誌編集長

掲載資料のご提供を感謝致します

稲吉デザイン企画室
西村画廊
富山県立近代美術館
フジテレビギャラリー